A Surprised Queenhood
in the New Black Sun

OTHER BOOKS BY ANGELA JACKSON

A
Surprised
Queenhood
in the
New Black Sun

The Life & Legacy of
GWENDOLYN BROOKS

Angela Jackson

Beacon Press
Boston

Beacon Press
Boston, Massachusetts
www.beacon.org

Beacon Press books
are published under the auspices of
the Unitarian Universalist Association of Congregations.

20 19 18 17   8 7 6 5 4 3 2 1

This book is printed on acid-free paper that meets the uncoated paper
ANSI/NISO specifications for permanence as revised in 1992.

Text design and composition by Kim Arney

FRONTIPIECE: Photo courtesy of Nora Brooks Blakely.

Library of Congress CIP Data is available for this title.
ISBN: 9780807025048 (hardcover : alk paper)
ISBN: 9780807025055 (e-book)

"I am moving. I am not still. I am ready
to be ready."

—GWENDOLYN BROOKS
from "The Near-Johannesburg Boy"

Contents

CHAPTER ONE

"Grant Me a Voice, and Speaking Eyes"

It was an indelible announcement written in black and white for all to see. The first nationally published poem of Gwendolyn Brooks's appeared in *American Childhood*, in October 1930, when she was only thirteen years old. Earlier, at eleven, she'd published four poems in a local neighborhood paper, the *Hyde Parker*, foreshadowing her brilliance. It was a brilliance that would shine through decades and across nations, bedazzling and impacting hundreds of poets and millions of audiences, in all walks of life.

Gwendolyn was a black teenager living on a quiet street in Chicago's Bronzeville neighborhood at 4332 South Champlain Avenue, where her family had lived since she was four years old.

Bronzeville, the name coined by an editor of a black newspaper, the *Chicago Bee*, was named for the color of the area's inhabitants. In those days, Bronzeville proper stretched from Thirty-First to Thirty-Ninth, and from State Street to Cottage Grove. It was a jewel of colored masses in a segregated space. The people were too often poor and illiterate, but they were also industrious and dignified, creative in music, language, dance, and style. They were the salt of the earth and birds who managed to fly with cramped wings. Gwendolyn, ever observant, settled in to learn the ways of her people, the geography and genius of Afro-America.

Hers was a protected space guarded by father and mother. She and her brother, Raymond, were nurtured and shielded by their father, David Brooks, a janitor at McKinley Music Company, and by their mother, Keziah Wims Brooks, a former schoolteacher who had given up working in the classroom to guide her own children. Gwendolyn was loved.

It was 1930 when she made her national debut. The world was just entering the Great Depression. But Gwendolyn didn't feel depressed. She was buoyed by dark ink on the pages of *Writer's Digest*, which she discovered at age thirteen. She reveled in the company of other writing souls who were on the same quest as she—to have their expressions published. She learned to send her work out, to include a self-addressed stamped envelope so that it might be returned when it was rejected. For rejection would and did come. She sent poems and stories out. She got them back. Her desk was her headquarters. But one day the letter she had been waiting for, a letter of acceptance, did come. At that moment, she was deliciously light-headed and light-hearted. Her first poem, "Eventide," was published in a national magazine. No doubt, her family celebrated her. She basked in her first victory, her announcement to the world.

When the sun sinks behind the mountains,
And the sky is besprinkled with color,
And the neighboring brook is peacefully still,
With a gentle, silent ripple now and then;
When the flowers send forth sweet odors,
And the grass is commonly green,
When the air is tranquilly sweet,
And children flock to their mothers' sides,

Then worry flees and comfort presides
For all know it is welcoming evening.

Of course, there were no mountains in Chicago—except for the mountains of clouds in the sky a young Gwendolyn was fond of studying. And no brook ran down Champlain Avenue. But Gwendolyn had learned, in her extended reading, about these natural wonders, and her imagination soaked up the solace of nature's beauty. Her experience in the Brooks household provided the template for the comforts of a "welcoming" home.

She was a pretty girl in her darksome way. And she was in love. She was always in love. Words and books were the love of her young life. Who would have thought that a baby girl born to David and Keziah Brooks in the dining room of her grandparents' two-story, single-family home at 1311 North Kansas Avenue in Topeka, Kansas, on June 7, 1917, would so soon become a published poet? Her parents, having migrated to Chicago earlier, had returned to Topeka for her birth. Gwendolyn was born during the Great War across the ocean, but she must have felt the reverberations of a world in conflict as she grew up. Negro soldiers were deemed unfit to fight by US commanders, so they battled under a French flag and returned home as heroes. She would become used to the theme of war. She was in touch with it, even in her little corner of the world.

Gwendolyn wrote poems a long time before she was published. She would sit on the top of the back steps and dream in poetry about the magic of sky and the mysteries of her future. She wrote a poem a day from the time she was eleven. Sometimes two or three. She was devoted to her poetry because her mother believed in her ability, her gift for it. When she was seven, she showed her mother her page of rhymes. Her mother was overjoyed, excited at the possibility of a poetic daughter who would conquer the segregated world with elegant and eloquent language. She, a schoolteacher, knew how important it was to achieve in letters.

"You're going to be the lady Paul Laurence Dunbar!" Keziah Wims Brooks exclaimed. And Gwendolyn believed this because her mother had said it was so. Her mother would do all that she could to make it happen. For example, early on Gwendolyn did not have to do chores.

Then later she dusted, swept, did some laundry, and washed dishes. But her mother carried the work of the household. Her mother sang "Brighten the Corner Where You Are" as she went about her work for her gifted child. Gwendolyn, with pen in hand, brightened her own corner in her little room of her own.

When she was in her early teens, her father gave her a desk of her own that he got from McKinley's. It was a desk full of compartments where she kept notebooks that she'd been writing in since she was eleven and special books like "the Emily books," L. M. Montgomery's books about a Canadian girl who, like Gwendolyn, wanted to be a writer. Of course, she kept *The Complete Paul Laurence Dunbar*.

When Gwendolyn wasn't writing, she was reading. Even at Christmas, she read. She sat near the Christmas tree and re-read the same book on that holy day: *The Cherry Orchard*, by Marie Battelle Schilling, a gift from Kayola Moore, her Sunday school teacher at Carter Temple Colored Methodist Episcopal Church. Gwendolyn would sit amid tinsel and gold, under a star-topped tree, and lose herself in the same book each year. Or did she find herself in the same book? Did she find herself in any story or poem—a vibrant, vivid, adventuresome self who taught her to live more confidently, at least in her mind? She only had a few friends on her short block.

She was a dark-skinned girl at the time when being a decidedly dark girl was not the most desirable thing to be. Black people, worldly-wise, sang, "If you're white / You're all right. If you're yellow / You're mellow. If you're brown / Stick around. If you're black / Get back. Get back. Get back." Gwendolyn understood the color code. She was bright that way. At the time her first poem was chosen for publication, she was not the most popular girl in any part of Negro society. But her self-esteem did not depend on others choosing her. She chose herself. Rejection hurt, but she had early on fallen in love with her own color because her parents, by their love of her and her brother, had taught her to love the totality of herself.

On her block, Gwendolyn was known. Even if she spent most of her time in the house, in her room at her desk, writing poems and stories and reading sometimes two books a day, she belonged. At school it was a different matter.

When she went to grammar school, to Forrestville Elementary School, outside her immediate neighborhood, she encountered teasing every other day about her complexion. Her classmates called her "Ole' Black Gal." At the time, most of the kids believed everything black was bad—a black heart, a black mood, a black knight, a dark design.

In describing herself as she was in her early teens, she said she was "timid to the point of terror, silent, primly dressed, AND DARK. The boys did not mind telling me that this was the failing of failings."[1] Gwendolyn withstood the insults but noticed the reverence her classmates had for the light-skinned girls.

The boys were drawn to light-skinned girls like magnets. They fawned over Rose Hurd, Eleanor Griffin, Rebecca Dorsey, and Gwendolyn's friend Ida Briscoe. These girls had boyfriends. Gwendolyn did not garner the attention of young Negro males until later, when she conversed with Joseph Quinn, light-skinned Herman Lawrence, Theries Lindsey, and more seriously dated one Kenyon Reid.[2] She had the consolation of and preference for books and her own creative impulse. Because of her interests and temperament—and especially her color—she did not fit in at Forrestville Elementary School. She learned that lightness was one crucial way that Negro society established the worth of its members.

The length and texture of the hair was also important to popularity. It had to be long and curly, and it was best if it did not need a hot comb to be straight or free from kinks. That was Good Hair. Gwendolyn did not have Good Hair. The wardrobe had to be fine, as well, reflecting the economic station of the parents—professional men like lawyers, doctors, politicians or porters and postal workers.[3] To have a schoolteacher for a mother was a boon. But Gwendolyn's mother was retired, and the family did not have the extra income anymore.

To top it all off, Gwendolyn was not athletic. She did not tumble and jump with ease. She had few social graces. She did not know how to make witty repartee and coin new phrases. Her classmates kept up the insults. One of Gwendolyn's earliest extant poems seems to be a response to personal slights and insults.

FORGIVE AND FORGET

If others neglect you,
Forget; do not sigh,
For, after all, they'll select you,
In times by and by,
If their taunts cut and hurt you,
They are sure to regret

And, if in time, they desert you,
Forgive and forget.

Gwendolyn's answer to the cruelty and insensitivity of young schoolmates was the perfect response she learned in the Sunday school she attended every week—a Christian, turn-the-other-cheek answer, reflecting a belief that things would be right by and by. It was a deeply held belief among African Americans as well. This belief, in Gwendolyn's mind, extended to whites, as well. She was working her life out in the privacy of her poetry.

Think of the pain of a sensitive black girl, beloved at home and snubbed at school, taunted in this way, at best ignored, at worst maligned. The hurt of it ran like a central seam in the garment of her writing. It would later inform her worldview and hold it together.

But as a student, she searched for a place to fit her dark self. She went to three different high schools in this effort.

Her first was the predominantly white Hyde Park Branch, at 6220 South Stony Island, where it was said the best students went. Gwendolyn hated her experience there, though. She felt isolated because she *was* isolated. She was a black canoe in a sea of whiteness. She was ignored, invisible to all but a few white boys, she would say later, who took an unreciprocated liking to her. Was she interesting to them because she was dark skinned and seemed exotic? Was her black skin alluring as forbidden fruit?

Gwendolyn packed up her books and headed to the all-black Wendell Phillips Academy on 244 East Pershing Road, at Thirty-Ninth Street, not too far from her home. She was hungry for a learning experience among her own people. A girl who lived next door to her on Forty-Third and Champlain had sworn up and down that Gwendolyn would "have a ball" at Wendell Phillips with its rich, black social life. But she didn't have a ball. She wasn't a have-a-ball person who knew the latest dances, partied on the weekends, played Post Office and Kiss the Pilla. She wasn't fast, athletic, stylishly dressed, or light skinned with long hair.

The last high school, from which she graduated, was Englewood High School, at 6201 South Stewart Street. Because she didn't live within the school's district, she used the address of one of her few friends in order to attend. Englewood was not solidly white like Hyde Park or wholly black like Wendell Phillips. It was mixed, though the majority of the students were white. But she did not feel so much like an outsider there. Still, no one ever said, "Hey, Gwen, are you coming to the party tomorrow night?"

No one ever said, "Girl, didn't we have a ball last Saturday night!"

Certainly no one ever said, "Oh, you're a doll!"

Or, "Heaven must be missing an angel."

But something romantic happened at Englewood, all the same. It was said that "when a white boy of affluent family flirted with her in class, he was threatened by a black boy who had a hitherto-controlled 'crush' on her."[4] What did Gwendolyn make of that scene? She blushed, no doubt mortified.

At Englewood High School three teachers recognized her talent for poetry and writing in general. Ethel Hurn in history and Margaret Harris in journalism encouraged her directly, and Horace Williston in American poetry encouraged her as well. Gwendolyn had tried to be published in the school paper but was rejected; then she turned in a book review—written in verse—of *Janice Meredith*, by Paul

Leicester Ford, which Gwendolyn had only half read because she hated it so. Hurn was greatly impressed with her writing and said Gwendolyn "had a future." Gwendolyn earned an A and her teacher's continued interest.

Concurrently, she joined the journalism club, and teacher Margaret Harris also believed in her. She had run into her on the bus one day and told Gwendolyn she thought she had talent. Gwendolyn was embarrassed to be singled out in public on the bus. But at home, in the safety of her room, she reveled in the encouragement. From Miss Harris in the journalism club she learned the W's—who, what, when, where, why. She also developed a discerning eye, which would help shape her life's work.

So three white teachers offered her plums of encouragement. There was no black teacher at the school, but Gwendolyn read about the ideas of other African Americans in the *Chicago Defender*. It was the most popular newspaper about Negro life at the time, and the most respected. An honored guest in many black homes, in truth, it had prompted many African Americans to vacate the cruelties and limitations of the South and seek out the opportunities and promise of the cities of the North.

Founded in 1905 by Robert Abbott and situated at Twenty-Fourth and Michigan Avenue, the *Defender* was sold by Pullman porters at stop-off points in towns, cities, and hamlets throughout the South. It was the town crier of the national black community and kept black people everywhere in touch with the black condition. It raised a hue and cry about the lynching in the South, reporting in great detail. It highlighted job openings in factories and steel mills in the North, and recruited workers for those jobs. It offered visions of life in domestic service and career advancement for the educated.

In addition, the *Defender* offered details of Negro social life—weddings, funerals, engagements, graduations, parties, recitals, musical venues, and athletic competitions. Charitable organizations, fraternities, sororities, and social clubs were highlighted. It was the *Chicago Defender*'s David Kellum who founded the Bud Billikin Back to School

Parade, an institution on Chicago's South Side that attracts hundreds of thousands onlookers and participants from across the city today.

Gwendolyn aspired to publish poetry in the pages of the *Chicago Defender*. She wanted to publish there as Langston Hughes did. On August 18, 1934, when Gwendolyn was seventeen, the following poem appeared in the pages of this national organ:

TO THE HINDERER

Oh, who shall force the brave and brilliant down?
There's no descent for him who treads the stars.
What else shall he care for mortal hate or frown?
He shall not care. His bright soul knows no bars.

Take his weak frame and twist it to your will.
Strive to discourage and to make him fall;
Oh, make him suffer! Cause his tears! But still
Shall not his spirit rise and vanquish all?

What things the Power buried in the skies
Of man's attempt to bruise and hinder man?
What pity has that Force for our poor cries
When crude destruction is our foremost plan.

Was "To the Hinderer" a hidden response to the chilly racism she'd encountered at Hyde Park Branch School, or a response to editors who were cold to her submissions she'd begun to send out? Or did the poem address, in its velvet-wrapped way, the society at large, surrounding Bronzeville and inside Bronzeville? Gwendolyn's was a gifted mind answering back with subtlety.

She would continue to send poetry to the *Chicago Defender*, which published her writings on the uselessness of fame, the bliss of friendship, quarrels. These were mature considerations for an adolescent girl. In four years, she published seventy-five poems in the paper's Lights and Shadows column.

In September 1935, after completing high school, Gwendolyn went directly to the new Woodrow Wilson Junior College, which had just opened its doors at Sixty-Eighth and Wentworth. She would graduate in 1936. While at Wilson, Gwendolyn enjoyed friendships, worked hard at her studies, and wrote regularly. More and more, her work began to engage Negro people, the people of her community, and the world at large.

Bolstered by the openness of the college experience, the communion of friends, the recounting of events of the day over radio, newsreels, and in the newspaper, she gave a passionate and urgent cry in response to the Italian dictator Mussolini, ally to Hitler. She responded to the rumblings of a world soon to be at war on October 12, 1935, in yet another contribution to the *Chicago Defender*:

WORDS FOR MUSSOLINI
"Dark men must learn to bow to bright"
How many, many times a flesh
of black has masked a soul of white.
Lord, Lord, I ask this gift of You!!
Grant me a voice, and speaking eyes.
That the quick-throbbing truth I know
May reach the deeps of earth and skies.

I want to tell them all in words
Shining and hard, and very cold,
This message that I know is Yours—
Else whence the richness of its gold?
I want to tell them that the sod
Is drab and deeply dark of hue,
Yet their material nourishment
From out the hated blackness grew.

The rose whose sweets they cherish sprang
From that same blackness they despise.
A hundred times I beg of You—
Grant me a voice, and speaking eyes.

Thus, Gwendolyn pleaded with eloquence and fire. She implored God for "a voice, and speaking eyes." And she would have these two major gifts.

Even though Gwendolyn herself demonstrated some ambivalence about the color of her skin and the color of her soul, she turned her gifts on intraracial conflicts of self-acceptance and self-love. Having gained perspective through age, experience, and self-confidence, she rebuked self-hate over and over again.

In a poem that she noted was "to be published in *Opportunity*," the journal of the Urban League, she scoffed at the woman who wrote on a job application that Gwendolyn had "Negroid features, but they're finely spaced." Gwendolyn felt the apology in the qualifying conjunction "but." She would have better phrased the sentence, "I've Negroid features—and they're finely spaced."[5]

Gwendolyn celebrated "A Brown Girl" (April 8, 1936): "But there is one tall brown girl: How high and fine her head / Her mouth, how firm; her eyes how cool; / How straight and strong her tread: / As if to say, 'I have no fear.'" This poem is reminiscent of the celebratory poetry of the Harlem Renaissance, the Negro Renaissance stressing racial pride.

In print, Gwendolyn celebrated the beauty of Negroness, and she castigated intra-racial colorism. She was bold and public in her address. But Gwendolyn also created a handmade volume of unpublished poems dated July 23, 1936, shortly after she graduated from Woodrow Wilson Junior College. It would include poems written from 1935 to 1936. She entitled it *Songs After Sunset*, suggesting work composed in near darkness, in quietude, away from the business of the day. These "songs" are mostly love poems "both worldly (friendship, marriage, nature) and divine (animism, God, Nature)."⁶ These poems are profoundly private—and universal.

> WE
> *An old man said this thing to me:*
> *"The loveliest word of all is 'we.'"*

Gwendolyn had been keeping notebooks since she was eleven and named them for each year, except for 1932, which went missing. These notebooks were named variously *My Fancy Book*, *The Red Book* or *The Merry Book*, *The Blue Book of Verse*, *The Account Book*, and *Book of Thoughts*.

She was so devoted to writing in her notebooks that at one point her mother grew concerned. To divert Gwendolyn's attention, and save her eyesight and health, she poked her head into Gwendolyn's room one day.

"There's a big fire down the street," Keziah told her daughter.

"Yes," Gwendolyn said, and kept on writing. She was creating.

But her mother was her chief champion, taking her to a lecture and reading by the esteemed James Weldon Johnson, writer of "Lift Every Voice and Sing." He was also the author of *God's Trombones*, poems of sermons of Negro preachers; was the national secretary of the NAACP; and had been the United States consul to Venezuela. He was a Great Man. A Great Negro. Gwendolyn was tongue-tied at the thought of meeting him. She too wanted to do Great Things.⁷

Years before, in 1933, when she was sixteen, Gwendolyn had sent some of her poetry to James Weldon Johnson. He had been kind in his reply and had offered valuable, encouraging feedback and legitimate and constructive criticism. On August 30, 1937, he wrote to her:

My dear Miss Brooks:

I have read the poems you sent me last. Of them, I especially like Reunion and Myself. Reunion is very good, and Myself is good. You should, by all means, continue you[r] study and work. I shall always be glad to give you any assistance that I can.

Sincerely yours,
James Weldon Johnson

In addition, he wrote kind and insightful notes in the margins of the poems.

Dear Miss Brooks—You have an unquestionable talent and feeling for poetry. Continue to write—at the same time, study carefully the work of the best modern poets—not to imitate them, but to help cultivate the highest possible standard of self-criticism.

Then he offered meticulous and generous criticism of poems she had sent. The poems included "Once She Lived," "Decay," and "After-gloom," poems befitting a sensitive, young woman with a serious, even morbid, bent.

Gwendolyn took Johnson's responses to heart. They discussed eliminating unnecessary words and feeling free to break the rigidity of the measured form. She knew the works of certain Negro poets such as Langston Hughes and Countee Cullen. Now she turned her attention to T. S. Eliot, Ezra Pound, and e. e. cummings.

So the prospect of meeting James Weldon Johnson was thrilling.

Gwendolyn and her mother went to their church, Carter Temple Colored Methodist Episcopal Church, on the northwest corner of their block, to hear Johnson's lecture. Her mother was aggressive, pushy for her talented, shy child.

"She's the one who sent you all those wonderful poems!" Keziah enthused to Mr. Johnson.

He responded coldly. He was hoisted high inside of himself. He crossed his arms in front of his chest and lifted to full height. "I get so many of them, you knooow."

Gwendolyn felt her face go hot. Why had she supposed he'd be otherwise? He was, after all, a Great Man of Achievement.

Her meeting with poet-writer Langston Hughes was kinder. Again, her mother took her to a church. This time it was Metropolitan Community. They went to meet this Great Man of Letters, a poet in touch with the pulse of the people and the pulse of poetry itself. He laughed gently and warmly upon meeting Gwendolyn and her mother.

Ever dreamy-eyed and practical, Keziah Wims Brooks insisted that her daughter show Hughes her poems. He read them on the spot, then leaned forward and gazed directly at her. "You're very talented!" he exclaimed. "Keep writing! Someday you'll have a book published!"

He was a soft-spoken man, but his words had weight. Standing there in church, he provided a gospel of clarity and empathy. His friendship would follow Gwendolyn through the years.

After graduating from Wilson Junior College, Gwendolyn went in search of a job. Her family needed her. She could not live by poetry alone. She was nineteen years old, able-bodied, educated, and expected to work. She of the "voice and speaking eyes" was a natural reporter. She not only liked to observe clouds, as she did on the back porch, but also liked to study people. She loved to listen in on the gossip between neighbors. At thirteen, she reported all that she had seen and heard in her own handwritten rag, the *Champlain Weekly News*. It sold for five cents. The press of schoolwork had caused Gwendolyn to cease publication of her newspaper. Now, Dewey Jones, who edited the Lights and Shadows column of the *Chicago Defender*, where Gwendolyn's poems were printed almost weekly, encouraged her to interview for a job as a reporter on the paper. Gwendolyn wrote to publisher Robert Abbott, posthaste. His reply was welcoming. An appointment was set up.

Gwendolyn and her mother met Abbott with anticipation. At first he met them with welcome on his countenance. Quickly, though, the warmth turned to cold stone. He was abrupt. "If we hire you, you will have to be on time every day." The meeting was over. They were dismissed, and she did not hear from him again.[8]

Gwendolyn sensed she had met the stone wall of color prejudice. Robert Abbott was color-struck. That is what Negroes called his strict preference for light-skinned Negro women.

Not to be deterred from her journalistic instincts, Gwendolyn again published her own newspaper. This time it was mimeographed. The *News-Review* sold for a nickel. A remaining copy demonstrates that Gwendolyn was in touch with cultural affairs and current events. This issue included local news and a speech by associate justice of the US Supreme Court Hugo L. Black. Gwendolyn's brother, Raymond, contributed a cartoon of Justice Black, a former Klansman, saying, "I number among my friends many members of the colored race." Along with the quote is an image of a black man hanging from a tree.

Gwendolyn contributed a poem, a short story, and an editorial, as well as biographies of Negroes of achievement. She quoted Emily Dickinson, William Shakespeare, and the Reverend Harold Kingsley "on the endurance of blacks." There was a Negro authors quiz, including luminaries from the Harlem Renaissance.[9]

Young Gwendolyn was a race woman, but she had to get a job. She worked for spells in domestic service. She went to the Illinois State Employment Service, which sent her to the Mecca Flats Building at Thirty-Fourth and State Street. It was a nine-block walk from the Brooks household.

Opened initially as a hotel in 1893, the ninety-six-unit apartment complex, known as the Mecca, was built on the edge of the Black Belt for upwardly mobile Negroes. Its fame spread far and wide. The dream of it sparked the imaginations of children and adults all the way to the Deep South.

At the Mecca, Gwendolyn would work for a "spiritual adviser," E. N. French, who made huge sums of money off the dreams, desires, and longing of needy and sick people. Gwendolyn, with other workers, answered imploring letters and bottled so-called curative medicine for the charlatan. These bottles, meant to attract love and money and good health and the resolution of difficult situations, were delivered by Gwendolyn and others throughout the Mecca. Ever the observant reporter, Gwendolyn witnessed "murders, loves, lonelinesses, hates, jealousies. Hope occurred, and charity, sainthood, glory, shame, despair, fear, altruism."[10] The young poet became intimately acquainted with the vast edifice and its denizens.

She worked among this spectrum of dark humanity for four months, for eight dollars a week, a portion of which she contributed to the Brooks household. She kept the job out of necessity but had to let it go when the "spiritual adviser" wanted to promote her to associate pastor. It was a job that would have entailed some preaching on her part. Gwendolyn could deliver potions, but she wasn't to deliver false notions or preach promises made of air. She would store the Mecca and its members in the storehouse of her mind and call up the innumerable nuances years later, failing to create anything significant about the place, again and again, until many years later. For now she still lived at home and gathered life around her in her mind.

The Brooks household was as gentile and orderly as an Elizabethan garden with each stick of furniture, knickknack, doily, and child in its place. David Brooks, head of the family, sang in a rich baritone while he worked around the house after working at McKinley Music Company. He sang his songs and went about family life good-naturedly. He could fix anything. He fastened pipes and the rivulets of water ran down his strong, black arms while he fixed the plumbing. He nailed down loose floor boards; he yanked out bent nails. He made the world right. He had studied medicine for a year at Fisk University in Nashville. His studies had ended when he started a family. He welcomed his children and loved to fulfill his doctoring skills on them. He fed them spoonfuls of cod-liver oil. He sat by Gwendolyn and Raymond's bedside and spoke softly to whichever of them was sick. He had a beguiling bedside manner and knowledge gleaned from reading and black folk medicine. Gwendolyn thought her father made her times being sick and convalescent worthwhile.

Her mother, Keziah, was dutiful, performing chores with supreme efficiency. Her house was immaculate. Her children were scrubbed and lotioned. But she made no outward displays of affection. Yet all the household tasks she performed so cheerfully, the caring and encouraging words, her vigorous pursuit of her children's excellence, were proof of a deep maternal love.

By the 1930s, when Gwendolyn was a precocious preteen and teenager, she observed all manner of people, dressed in their best, strolling down the avenue, on their way to Forty-Seventh and South Parkway. In the vicinity of the Brookses' household, seven blocks away, vendors lined Forty-Seventh Street. The Regal Theater, which opened its doors in 1928, was nearby, part of a complex that also included the Savoy Ballroom, a Walgreens, and the South Center Department Store, with the Madame C. J. Walker Beauty Salon and Walker School of Beauty opened. The complex was built by Harry M. and Louis Engelstein, white men in pursuit of the Negro dollar. When Negroes had money, they spent it in their community because they had to. There was nowhere else to go.

The Regal Theater was magnificent, an alluring palace of marble floors and decorative cornices. Its seat covers were imported from North Africa. Its chandeliers, made of crystal, came from Belgium. Artwork suggesting Moorish castles under a North African sky of stars enclosed the space. The Regal was the place to be. And all of Bronzeville, the classes of the Black Metropolis, went there. The Regal Theater attracted the whole of the Negro community because it attracted the headliners of the day, as well as rising local talents. It offered films as well, like *Flying Down to Rio* with Chicago's Etta Moten Barnette, whose husband, Claude, was the head of the Associated Negro Press. It showed features with Bette Davis, Katherine Hepburn, and Spencer Tracy. Its live stage shows featured comedians and performers that included Paul Robeson, Duke Ellington, Louis Armstrong, Ethel Waters, Count Basie, zoot-suiter Cab Calloway, banana-leaved Josephine Baker, and tap dancer Bill Robinson. Gwendolyn, her mother, and brother went to see movies at the Regal Theater that stirred Gwendolyn's romantic fantasies, and she went to see live stage shows that she would write about later.

Within a four-block radius of the central site of Bronzeville—Forty-Seventh and South Parkway—was Providence Hospital, at

Fifty-First just off South Parkway, staffed by Negro doctors and nurses. There was also the George Cleveland Hall Branch Library on Forty-Eighth and Michigan Avenue, with its impressive collection of work on and by Negroes in the Vivian Harsh Research Collection of Afro-American History and Literature; the South Parkway Branch of the YWCA; and the Michigan Boulevard Garden Apartments. Each of these would be significant to Gwendolyn's life and work.

The NAACP Youth Council held its meetings at the YWCA building and, in 1937, Gwendolyn, at the urging of Lula Battle, her friend from Wilson, attended a meeting and joined the group. The council included an ambitious group of progressive, forceful, young intellectuals who would accomplish significant things. They were not leftists, but they pressed against the status quo of repression and poverty assigned to Negroes. Of the members, Joseph Quinn, head of the council, would become a teacher in California; Sarah Merchant, important to Gwendolyn in another way, would also become a teacher; George Coleman Moore, a teacher as well as a writer; Theries Lindsey, a friend from Wilson days, would become an attorney; and John H. Johnson would found and build a media empire that included *Ebony* magazine, *Jet, Negro Digest/Black World* magazine, *Ebony Jr.*, Fashion Fair cosmetics, and the Ebony Fashion show. Last, but not least, was Gwendolyn's friend Margaret Taylor Goss, who became a renowned painter, writer, cofounder of the South Side Community Arts Center, and founder/director of the DuSable Museum of African American History.[11]

The camaraderie among NAACP Youth Council members was intense, and Gwendolyn entered a more active and activist moment in her life. Thelma Johnson, president of the council, and Margaret Goss created a sense of hospitality and community for the members. They socialized together and held dances and gatherings, but they also engaged in meaningful and substantive talk. Gwendolyn was still reserved, but she began to blossom in a space suited for her passionate interior. She entered into the activism of the group, protesting against lynching. Council members wore paper shackles around their necks, symbolizing the lynch rope, and marched, carrying placards protesting the wrong done to the Scottsboro boys in Alabama. And Gwendolyn went to dances and danced. She was accepted as a writer, a thinker, and a committed race woman. Her peers in the council were young, gifted, and Negro, and it was the end of the 1930s in Chicago, in Bronzeville. She was finally one of the group.

Gwendolyn was a little girl during the Harlem Renaissance, which stretched well beyond New York. Being Negro was in. Negroness was even in vogue on Broadway in shows like *Shuffle Along* and whites in-filtrated Harlem to be entertained at nightclubs where light-skinned beauties danced in their glory. All this activity flurried in the air like flecks of smoke from a stupendous fire that was headquartered in Harlem but fanned out across the nation. It swirled down to a quiet street in Bronzeville and a young Negro girl named Gwendolyn. And in the 1930s, new embers of another Renaissance were starting to burn in Bronzeville. Chicago was the perfect place for another Renaissance. In the 1920s, Chicago's Black Belt had been the center of economic and political power for Negroes. This crucial power was based upon many institutions that had been established from 1890 to 1915, including a bank, a hospital, a YMCA, an infantry regiment, effective political organizations, lodges, clubs, professional baseball teams, social service institutions, five newspapers, and a number of small businesses.[12] Yet before there could be a flowering, there was a Depression to survive.

The Depression years (1929–1940) were felt in the Brooks home. Even though Negroes claimed often that they didn't feel the Depression because their community was always in a state of depression and just getting by, the Great Depression hit hard. There was mass unemployment—factory and mill layoffs, domestics lost their jobs. Twenty-five million men were out of work—both Negro and white.

After Franklin D. Roosevelt won the election, in 1932, lengthy relief lines for government assistance lined the street. There were work programs instituted to offer employment to hungry people who were looking for more than a handout. They wanted a leg up, some boot straps to pull themselves up by.

In the Brooks household, father David often brought home twenty-five dollars a week during the best of times at the McKinley Music Company. During the worst of times, during the Depression, he brought home eight to ten dollars a week. Gwendolyn's parents quarreled over money and even separated for a time, during which David took Gwendolyn and her brother, Raymond. But the family was reunited, and David took on a second job, house painting. It was during those trying times that Keziah Wims Brooks changed the family menus from lamb, hamburger patties, and chicken with potatoes and vegetables to beans, beans, and more beans. They ate the beans without complaining. Some people had less. Yet whatever was on their table, they welcomed to it hungry strangers who knocked at their door.

After dinner, David Brooks would spend quality time with his children. He had a deep love of books and read to them Paul Laurence Dunbar poems. He sang songs to them and he told them stories. He told them about his father, who had been a slave. Once his father had achieved freedom, he moved to Oklahoma. He was enterprising and proved to be a successful farmer. In turn, his white neighbors grew envious and poisoned his mules and horses. So he moved. From this family story, Gwendolyn learned about the poisonous power of envy and knew it was something to guard against. Her father told them all the things he had seen in the world, especially the events of the summer of 1919. The Depression that hit some years later was hard, but the Red Summer of 1919 was harder.

David and Keziah had brought newborn Gwendolyn from Kansas to Chicago just two years before the Red Summer, when postwar race riots swept American cities. Hundreds, mostly black people, were killed. In most cases, whites had attacked Negro people. In Chicago, whites got more than they bargained for: the blacks fought back. Robert Abbott of the *Chicago Defender* had exhorted black people in a 1915 slogan, "If you must die, take at least one with you." (Never mind that Abbott was the same man who treated Gwendolyn coldly during a job interview because her complexion was not light enough.) Negroes in Chicago did just that. Chicago was what white poet Carl Sandburg called "the Hog Butcher for the world." It could cut a man down. One had to be tough to survive in Chicago.

Gwendolyn Brooks came from this community of tough-minded people. She would sit at her desk now in the late 1930s, more mature, more conscious of herself and her world. Her calling was clear—to write, and that included writing about her surroundings. She was surrounded by life, by Bronzeville.

CHAPTER TWO

Visionaries

Young Gwendolyn's activism in the NAACP Youth Council embold-
ened her creative spirit, and her creativity and literary ambitions
walked hand-in-hand with her involvement with like-minded, serious,
young, progressive Negroes. The late 1930s and 1940s would signal
a period of enormous personal and artistic fulfillment. These satisfied
parts of her being were brought about directly not by her action as a
gifted individual but through her engagement in group activities. As
she embraced her activist and literary communities, the entire commu-
nity embraced her back.

After graduating from Woodrow Wilson Junior College, and during
her engagement with the NAACP, Gwendolyn was at war with herself
concerning her womanhood versus her art. She concluded, "But as for
happiness, / That comes with Love alone. / I guess."[1] But the balance
between womanly duties and fancies, and artistic pursuits persisted.
Yet Gwendolyn surrendered to her destiny as a poet and writer, and
she intelligently followed the path seemingly laid out for her.

Gwendolyn entered a new, critical phase of her writing when she
met her first and only truly serious beau, Henry Blakely Jr. She and
Henry talked poetry and shared books. They gazed into each other's
eyes and liked what they saw. He was a rich-brown, bespectacled young

man, tallish. She stood beside him and looked up into the future. She recognized his presence from her dreams as a young girl. He would be her husband and the father of her long-planned-for children. She believed her body was designed for children—and her mind for poetry.

Their meeting was auspicious. He heard from a friend, Sarah Merchant, that there was a girl who wrote poetry who went to the NAACP Youth Council. He wanted to meet her, so he stood in the doorway of the YWCA at Forty-Sixth and South Park, and Gwendolyn looked up and saw him. He was serious looking and bore himself with dignity. She smiled a secret smile as she observed the newcomer. She turned to her friend Margaret Taylor Goss, painter and poet, and said, "There is the man I'm going to marry."

Bold Margaret the Matchmaker yelled across the room at young Henry, "Hey, boy, this girl wants to meet you!"

"Love at first sight" is a phenomenon that poets and songwriters write about. It is legendary because it happened more so in a time before cynicism and casual sex. It is an experience for the innocent.

Gwendolyn and Henry were both twenty-one. It was 1938. They had enjoyed a year-long courtship of dating, going to the movies, sharing books and each other's poetry, kisses, and embraces. Gwendolyn was raised by a mother so religious that she wrote hymns. She raised Gwendolyn to be a "nice girl." Yet over the years, in the "Lights and Shadows" column of the *Chicago Defender*, Gwendolyn had revealed a passionate heart that constantly yearned after romantic love. Earlier than that, in her childhood dreams, she had fantasized about a loving man who would be the kind of doting father to her children that her own father was to her and her brother, Raymond. She wrote in a poem that she had longed for a tall, dark, and handsome man, with these strict physical stipulations. As she matured, she asked for a mate who was "kind." Henry Blakely was all of these.

They were deeply in love and wanted to be one in body as well as spirit. "Better to marry, than to burn," St. Paul said. Gwendolyn and Henry wanted to marry, but their parents, especially Henry's mother, argued that the couple was not yet ready for marriage and that her son was not yet mature enough for the responsibilities of maintaining a wife and household. But the fires of young love and the wisdom of destiny prevailed. Gwendolyn and Henry were wed a year after they first met, in the living room of the Brooks family home on that street in Bronzeville.

Over the course of the next few years, they lived in several apartments in Bronzeville. The first was a kitchenette in the Tyson building on Forty-Third and South Park; the second, a room at a Mrs. Sapp's; the third, a kitchenette at 6424 South Champlain, where their son, Henry III, or Hank, as he was called, was born on October 10, 1940. They then moved to a garage apartment at 5412 South Indiana, followed by a mice-ridden kitchenette at 623 East Sixty-Third, under the clattering "L" train, where they lived for seven years.

These experiences of living in kitchenette apartments and moving around the Black Metropolis trying to find a suitable place to settle in a segregated city with housing shortages would appear in her poetry and fiction. Both Gwendolyn and Lorraine Hansberry, in her play *A Raisin in the Sun*, would deal with the crucial issue of housing in their works.

Gwendolyn and Henry, in all of their apartments, enjoyed married life and the pleasures of guests, and they enjoyed reading and writing together. At times, the difficulties of finding adequate housing caused tension to run high in their marriage, enough to fuel brief break-ups. But their relationship was a good one. Henry, over time, wrote less, as he was the main breadwinner. He was happy to support his wife as a husband and as a fellow artist. He appreciated her giftedness. He sacrificed his talent for hers. He was an upright man and was determined to take care of his wife and child. But he did not believe she appreciated how hard he worked. He had a mind for business and would co-own an auto repair shop, but he also labored as a mechanic, a factory worker, and a truck driver.

Gwendolyn attempted to contribute to the young family's income by performing secretarial services and working at home writing radio scripts. These attempts were unsuccessful.

The apartment on Sixty-Third provided enriching street scenes, grist for Brooks's mill. She said, "If you wanted a poem, you had only to look out of a window."[2] On Sixty-Third Street, Gwendolyn and Henry were in the thick of things. After the birth of her son, in 1940, and the early years of devoting loving attention to her child, Gwendolyn was able to get a good measure of work done. Henry did not require that she put housewifery first. She was able to fit in her work.

She and Henry also enjoyed visitors, such as the playwright Ted Ward, who was their neighbor for a time on Sixty-Third. Ward's legendary drama *Big White Fog* opened in Chicago in 1938 at the Federal Theater Project. It was later staged in New York by the Negro Playwrights Company, which Ward founded with Paul Robeson and Langston Hughes, other left-leaning artists. Robeson would, in time, suffer enormously for his political views and outspokenness.

An avowed Communist, Ted Ward provided Gwendolyn with stimulating conversation. Ward was part of the South Side Writers Group, which included poet Frank Marshall Davis, editor Fern Gayden, sociologist St. Clair Drake, and Edward Bland, who would prove extremely significant to Gwendolyn and Henry Blakely's intellectual development.

The South Side Writers Group held its inaugural meeting, in May 1936, with a young Richard Wright at its head. The group included the aforementioned members, as well as a relocated Harlem Renaissance poet and writer, Arna Bontemps; young poet and Northwestern University student Margaret Walker; sculptor Marion Perkins, who was also a playwright and who would, in time, father poet/playwright Useni Eugene Perkins; Communist youth leader Claude Lightfoot; poet Robert Davis; and anthropology student Marian Minus. Occasionally, the legendary poet Fenton Johnson would join the group.

The group met for fewer than two years, but it had an intellectual ripple effect. Its bold intellectuality, grasp of social issues, and staunch view of reality through a Marxist lens cast a clear and grim picture of the circumstances of the people of Bronzeville. And Gwendolyn Brooks—poet—benefitted from that lens of social realism.

When the South Side Writers Group was winding down, in 1938, Gwendolyn was still active in the NAACP Youth Council. Her involvement as press and publicity person was put to good use on August 6 of that year when she sent a letter to Lady Katherine Simon, a British aristocrat and social activist who had spoken out against slavery and lynching.

> Dear Lady Simon:
>
> We, members of the Chicago Youth Council of the National Association for the Advancement of Colored People, recently observed in an American magazine, LIFE, a reference to your "great interest in life—the abolition of slavery in Africa and of lynching in the United States."
>
> May we express our sincere admiration! For this is our "great interest" too: our aim is to do all we can to stop lynching and racial discrimination. We cannot tell you how deeply we appreciate the earnest sympathy of such a person as yourself. These horrors do not touch you personally—yet you realize that the progress of civilization must of necessity be retarded as long as they exist.
>
> We would be pleased beyond measure to have an early reply from you, discussing more fully your "great interest."
>
> Yours truly, Gwendolyn Brooks,
> Press and publicity chairman,
> The Chicago Youth Council, NAACP

Lady Simon replied:

> Dear Miss Brooks,
>
> Your kind appreciation of any work I have done in regard to rousing public opinion against the two great iniquities of our time, Slavery and Lynching, has touched me very much. Injustice or oppression to ANY race rouses me to fierce indignation. I regard lynching to be entirely contrary

to a civilized sense of justice. If a man, Negro or white, does wrong he must bear being punished. But the law must investigate the crime and prove if the man is guilty. . . .

This exchange demonstrates how Gwendolyn and the Youth Council members believed themselves very much citizens of the world, able to speak directly, eyeball-to-eyeball, to others of any station. They stood on their inherent dignity as human beings. They were not the bowing, bumbling, comic Negroes depicted in popular films of the day. They moved in the world as modern men and women. They lacked monetary resources but enjoyed limited access beyond the confines of a segregated environment that was enriched by black imagination and élan.

Even before their marriage, Gwendolyn and Henry had been members of the Cre-Lit Club, along with Margaret Burroughs (formerly Goss). As a member of Cre-Lit, Gwendolyn would express her artistic questing. "Think how many fascinating documents there would be now, if all the great poets had written of what happened to them personally—and of the thoughts that occurred to them, no matter how ugly . . . fantastic . . . seemingly ridiculous," she wrote.[3] The Cre-Lit Club did not simply engage in poetry but was also studying the elements of drama in order to present plays and skits, though there is no record of these plans bearing fruit.

But that was all before the birth of baby Hank. Gwendolyn Brooks was born to be a mother and a poet. She gave herself over to motherhood. Her second child, a daughter named Nora, was born September 8, 1951.

Gwendolyn deeply adored her children. She was both affectionate and affirming. She memorized their every childhood charm and shared some delightful moments with readers of her autobiography years later. In those years of young motherhood, caring for her two offspring was of primary importance. There was a home-centered order to the lives of Gwendolyn and Henry, though she would attempt to write out in tiny spaces of time each day.

In 1941, a year after the birth of Hank, there came into Gwendolyn and Henry Blakely's lives through the NAACP Youth Council a life-changing person: Inez Cunningham Stark. Stark was white, wealthy, elegant of bearing and dress, well coiffed, and well educated. She was a reader for *Poetry* magazine, president of the Renaissance Society of the University of Chicago, and a believer in social justice in the arts. Stark believed that Negroes could write serious literature, poetry included. She stood for the cutting edge in the arts. And she was, as Gwendolyn described her, a rebel.

Despite the warnings and censure of fellow white socialites of the North Shore (the Gold Coast), who believed solely in the dangers of the Black Belt—and threats to Inez's safety—Inez proceeded with her artistic plan. She approached the well-known and highly visible NAACP for a list of members with a literary bent. The list included, of course, Gwendolyn and Henry but also Margaret Burroughs; William Couch; John Carlis, who would become a renowned visual artist; Margaret Danner (later Cunningham), who would become an associate editor of the prestigious *Poetry* magazine; critic Edward Bland; and, later, poet Robert Davis.

Stark conducted Wednesday evening poetry workshops at the South Side Community Art Center at 3831 South Michigan Avenue in the heart of Bronzeville. She would enter the room holding a pile of books and place the books on a table or pass them around the room. She would begin to read poetry from a designated volume. One book that she sometimes read from was *First Principles of Verse*, by Robert Hillyer. After she finished reading the introductory poem, the students would respond to it—its technical aspects, its style, its content. There was always excitement and energy. Then they would move to the poetry of workshop members.

Gwendolyn recounts, "The 'students' evaluated, criticized, praised, tore. They treated similarly their own precious creations, laboriously evolved during the seven days since the last meeting. Sometimes what we said to each other hurt or stung. We were all, those of us who remained after the first winnowing week, desperately earnest, and could not always be careful. Her [Inez Cunningham Stark] own expressed opinions were cool, objective, frank."[4]

The group continued for more than a decade under different names: the Chicago Poets' Class, the Visionaries, and the Creative Writing Forum. Whatever the workshop was called, it was an intense, stimulating, enriching, and productive experience for its participants, who would later publish poetry, fiction, articles, and criticism themselves. Stark gave them each a subscription to *Poetry* magazine.

She steered them away from clichés, wordiness, the arcane. She encouraged them to write about what they knew in language that was fresh and invigorated with invention. She did not impose her rules upon them. They had the final say over their own poems.

Gwendolyn engaged in deep conversations about poetry with fellow workshop member Margaret Danner. Margaret, who would not publish a volume until much later in life, probed Gwendolyn's growing technical virtuosity. For, indeed, Gwendolyn grew through Stark's poetry workshop and its extensive and exhaustive exploration of the techniques of the Moderns. She was cracking open the deeper secrets of English-language poetry and modernity. She also grew through the intellectual exchanges of ideas with fellow members, for they expanded her point of view. She was receiving a graduate-level education.

Members of the Visionaries sometimes visited Inez Stark's elegant apartment on the Gold Coast. Some were richly impressed by the trappings of her great wealth. When the group of young Negroes arrived at the residence, the doorman sent them around to the service elevator. He was roundly chastised by Inez for this display of disrespect toward her invited guests. The Visionaries were welcomed by the society of one far-thinking and privileged white woman.

The Inez Cunningham Stark workshop would lead to greater opportunities for Gwendolyn. She was leading a rich life but had her hands full as a wife, mother, and burgeoning writer.

And the world itself was about to change. On December 7, 1941, Japan staged a surprise attack on the Pearl Harbor naval base, in Hawaii. America declared war against Japan, Germany, and Italy the next day. Crucially, and for the first time, black men were deemed fit to fight in the US Army and were allowed to serve in the mess in the Navy. Able-bodied black men enlisted or were drafted to fight for the country that oftentimes did not allow them to vote, where they were denied the right to sit wherever they wanted in a public place, denied the rights to live where they wanted, to sleep where they wanted, to eat where they wanted, or to marry whomever they wanted.

The whole nation was involved in fighting the war, supporting the war effort, making ammunition and weapons, raising money, and conserving goods like sugar. Letters to and from the war zones were part of the way of life. Soldiers even wrote to strangers who were willing to respond, including Gwendolyn. These wartime correspondences would inform her poetry.

The presence in communities of soldiers on leave or waiting to be shipped out would also affect civilians. The sense of life itself felt urgent. Yet the war had brought increased employment to black people, white women, and others traditionally not considered for jobs held by white men. White men, of course, had held the desirable white-collar jobs and black men filled the factories, slaughterhouses, and canneries. Now, black people from the Deep South, including Mississippi, Alabama, Arkansas, and Louisiana, headed to Chicago to answer the call for war jobs and open employment. In 1930, the black population was 234,000. In 1940, it was 278,000, 8.2 percent of the city's population. By 1950, in the postwar years, the black population had swelled to 492,000 or 13.6 percent of the city's population.

The rise of women was reflected not only by the new jobs they held during the war but also by their status in the entertainment world. Audiences at the Regal Theater were entertained regularly by the International Sweethearts of Swing, a predominantly black orchestral group from Piney Woods, Mississippi. Audiences laughed and forgot their troubles during the comedic monologues of Jackie "Moms" Mabley, irreverent and risqué and a departure from previous entertainment. She was not slapstick. She was sharp-witted and sexual as an "Ole Lady" looking for a young man.[5]

Most significant in terms of women in entertainment was a new songstress growing in popularity. Her name was originally Ruth Jones, but her managers rechristened her Dinah Washington. Her crinkly voiced magic earned her the title "Queen of the Blues."[6] Listening to "What a Difference a Day Makes" and "This Bitter Earth," it is easy to understand why Gwendolyn wrote her important poem "Queen of the Blues." Gwendolyn, who attended the Regal, was likely familiar with the classy and elegant vocalist. There is also some irony to Gwendolyn's poem having the same moniker as Dinah Washington, considering that the "Queen of the Blues" was a bawdy, shimmy-shaking woman, yearning to be treated with the dignity of a queen.

Even as the citizens of the Black Belt began to thrive economically in the postwar years, the increase in population exacerbated the existing housing problems. Negroes were confined to a limited territory because of housing restrictions. Landlords thrived on Negro misery because they cut up decent, large apartments to create small kitchenette units that black families were crammed inside. In addition, white people could enter the Black Belt at will, whereas black people were denied entry to their side of the world. As late as 1950, less than 1 percent of the entire police department was black.[7] Black people were penned in to a limited territory and white policemen were their overseers.

But black life was spiced with music, and black folks went dancing at the well-known nightclubs in the tight community. There was the famous Savoy, attached to the Regal Theater on Forty-Seventh and South Parkway; the long-lasting Club DeLisa, on Fifty-Fifth and State Street; and the Rhumboogie "Boogie" Club, around Fifty-Fifth and South Park; as well as other clubs providing places of relaxation and psychic release. Impressive Negro entertainers were at these night spots as well.

Black people made the best of a bad situation. East Forty-Seventh Street thrived, and on any night a visiting star like Lena Horne could be seen strolling out of a club. The world was at war, and the nation was tied up in the war effort, but according to Gwendolyn, "1941 through

1949 was a party era. Partying now was most important."[8] They so-
cialized, drank spirits, and engaged in marvelous debates at people's
homes. Evelyn Ganns gave bountiful soirees in her spacious home on
Drexel Boulevard. She was one of the first Negroes to buy property on
the Boulevard. The food and drink was served liberally and the talk was
also. They talked excitedly about the problem of race, Jim Crow, Down
South and "Up South," and how to solve these problems and other so-
cial ills. Margaret Goss gave parties where the food was simpler, less ex-
pensive (black bread and cheese), but the conversation might last until
deep into the next day. Gwendolyn described Goss as "a rebel [living]
up from the root." She was far more interested in ideas than superficial
social manners. To get the party going, sometimes participants pooled
their money and went out for additional refreshments.

The list of guests at these gatherings might include Paul Robeson;
Frank Marshall Davis; actor Robert Davis; artists Hughie Lee Smith,
Charles White, Elizabeth Catlett (who would later take up residence
in Mexico only to be denied reentry to the United States to attend an
artists' conference at Northwestern University), Eldzier Cortor, and
Charles Sebree; pianist Earl Hines; Thomas Dorsey; and the dancer
and anthropologist Katherine Dunham. "My husband and I knew
writers, knew painters, and dancers and actresses, knew photographers
galore," wrote Gwendolyn.[9]

Indeed, life at 623 East Sixty-Third Street was full. To cap it
off, Gwendolyn and Henry gave a party for Langston Hughes. They
squeezed approximately one hundred people into the two-room kitch-
enette. "Best party I've ever been given!" Hughes exclaimed at the blues
music, the congenial atmosphere, the intelligent talk. He must have
enjoyed the hospitality of the Blakelys so much that he dropped in
unexpectedly years later at dinner time. He happily shared their meal
of mustard greens, ham hocks, and candied sweet potatoes.

Life was not all sweetness, however. Gwendolyn and Henry would
share a tragic connection to the war. Edward Bland was a young critic
who, with his brother Alden, Gwendolyn credited with "teaching
[her] and Henry how to think."[10] Edward's intellectual prowess was

ever evolving. He began as a Marxist while working at the post office, as had Richard Wright, and developed a vision critical of the black middle class, which he did not believe availed itself of its opportunity to be broader in scope, indeed international. Later, Edward presented at the Wednesday evening Inez Cunningham Stark poetry workshop his theory on the Negro artist. He believed that the Negro existed in a pre-individualistic state, thinking of him or herself only in terms of race. Negroes, he believed, saw humanity as races, not as individuals. Members of the poetry workshop vigorously argued both sides of this point.

During World War II, Edward served as a sergeant and was killed on a mission in Germany. Gwendolyn initiated the idea for the Edward Bland Memorial Fellowship Prize, to be funded by the South Side Community Art Center group. Each member paid fifty dollars a year for three years to poets selected by the editors of *Poetry* magazine. It was an act of enormous generosity for these poets and writers of limited means.

The Visionaries group was a conduit for experimentation and achievement. In 1943, at Inez Cunningham Stark's encouragement, Gwendolyn submitted poems to the Midwestern Writers Conference at Northwestern University. Later that year, Alice Manning Dickey, director of the conference, came to Gwendolyn and Henry's apartment to tell her that she had won the conference prize. She won the award in 1944 and 1945 as well. When Gwendolyn was suddenly named winner in 1945 for "Gay Chaps at the Bar," a poem about Negro soldiers, she was too stunned to move at the ceremony. All eyes were on her. She sat while the audience was amazed to learn that a young Negro woman had won three times in a row. (The judge was Paul Engle, Iowan poet and professor, who would teach Margaret Walker at the University of Iowa.) Then the applause rose.

But for Gwendolyn, the good news did not end with these prestigious regional prizes. As a result of her award in 1943, an editor for the Alfred Knopf Publishing Company sent her a request for poems for a possible book. Excitedly, Gwendolyn presented a manuscript of forty poems—love poems, war poems, nature poems, patriotism poems, "prejudice" poems.[11] The editor, Emily Morrison, responded with a rejection. She suggested that Gwendolyn resubmit a full volume of poems about black life. Gwendolyn, rebuffed by the rejection of the editor who had solicited her work, sent nineteen "Negro poems" to Harper & Brothers. She did not risk another rejection from Knopf. Harper & Brothers accepted the work and encouraged Gwendolyn to take the time she needed to write. It is interesting to note that editors at Knopf and at Harper & Brothers were most drawn to the poems about the people of Bronzeville, the area that held Gwendolyn's devoted regard as a poet.

When Harper & Brothers accepted Gwendolyn's work, the editor, Elizabeth Lawrence, sent Gwendolyn a letter from an affirming reader whom they had asked to evaluate the work. The reader was Richard Wright.

Wright had left Chicago in May 1937 but maintained an interest in his adopted city, where he lived after growing up in Mississippi. He asked his friend Margaret Walker to send him newspaper clippings of a notorious crime that had occurred in the city, which he later used as the seed for his inflammatory protest novel *Native Son*. *Native Son* was a critical success and a best seller, and launched Wright as the reigning Negro writer. And he was published by Harper & Brothers. When asked to evaluate Gwendolyn's work, Wright, novelist and a poet himself, responded to his editor, Edward C. Aswell:

> Thanks for letting me read Gwendolyn Brooks' poems. They are hard and real, right out of the central core of Black Belt Negro life in urban areas. I hope she can keep on saying what she is saying in many poems.
>
> There is no self-pity here, not a striving for effect. She takes hold of reality as it is and renders it faithfully. There is not so much an exhibiting of Negro life to whites in these poems as there is an honest human reaction to the pain that lurks so colorfully in the Black Belt. A quiet, but hidden malice runs through most of

them. She really catches the pathos of petty destinies, the whimper of the wounded; the tiny accidents that plague the lives of the desperately poor, and the problem of color prejudice among Negroes. There are times when open scorn leers through. Only one who has actually lived and suffered in a kitchenette could render the feeling of lonely frustration as well as she does—of how dreams are drowned out by the noises, smells, and the frantic desire to grab one's chance to get a bath when the bathroom is empty. Miss Brooks is real and so are her poems.[12]

Richard Wright went on to praise a number of poems that captured the frustrations and triumph of Negro life. The only poem he objected to was "the mother," because he did not feel that there was any poet who could make the subject of abortion fit for poetry. (But Gwendolyn kept the poem in and read it widely, and thousands of women, especially, were and are grateful for its inclusion.) Wright quibbled with the title of the book, thinking it too Chicago-specific. Finally, Wright believed that the poems themselves lacked a personal feel, and he suggested that she write a long poem that conveyed her own feelings or twice as many short poems that did the same. He concluded the letter by encouraging Harper & Brothers to help Gwendolyn promote her book because hers was an important voice.

Thus Gwendolyn, who had not yet met Richard Wright face-to-face, would get to know him in an exchange of letters that began in 1945, when she wrote to thank him for his support with Harper & Brothers and for the constructive criticism he had offered her. Her letters of appreciation to Wright were appropriately self-effacing and respectful of his status as the more accomplished writer.

When Harper & Brothers conditionally accepted Gwendolyn's work, her editor, Elizabeth Lawrence, advised her to take her time in creating additional poems to flesh out the manuscript. But for Gwendolyn, acceptance was a cause for artistic acceleration. She swore off her and Henry's regular Saturday movies and weekend parties. Instead, she worked quietly in their little apartment, writing eleven sonnets and the long "personally felt" poem "The Sundays of Satin Legs Smith." Heart pounding, she mailed the manuscript.

The response was swift. An anxious Gwendolyn ran into the "community bathroom," which she shared with everyone on the floor of her apartment building, and locked the door and tore open the letter from Harper & Brothers. She read with urgency. Yes! Her work was officially accepted. She later recalled the response to news as "Pandemonium. The Crowd—my 'crowd'—went wild. My family, my friends, my neighbors, thanked heaven and Harper's."[13]

The entirety of Bronzeville and beyond was abuzz with the announcement of Gwendolyn's first published volume, *A Street in Bronzeville*. In the Off the Book Shelf column of the February 24, 1945, issue of the *Chicago Defender*, the forthcoming collection was mentioned with pride. Then, on August 18, its publication was heralded with a lovely photograph of young Gwendolyn. *A Street in Bronzeville* was described as "a book of ballads, blues, and portraits-in-verse."

The publication of *A Street in Bronzeville* would indicate that Gwendolyn had served a solid and extended apprenticeship in the pages of the *Chicago Defender* and other publications, but she had proven her meddle in the strenuous and continuous Inez Cunningham Stark workshop, the group of Visionaries. The workshop had edged her into an increased sophistication of intellect and technique, providing an environment of frank, constructive criticism and bold, new ideas. That she and her husband, Henry Blakely, were both members would enhance their marriage and their life as a couple in a rich arena of gifted young Negro artists. But Gwendolyn was soon to be more than a favorite daughter of Bronzeville. She would become a bright and shining star of national consequence.

CHAPTER THREE

A Light and Diplomatic Bird

"We are each other's harvest," Gwendolyn Brooks would write years later. But the years from 1945 to 1949 were a time of laboring and significant harvest with the publication of two volumes of her work, *A Street in Bronzeville* and *Annie Allen*. With these slim, eloquent books, Gwendolyn would establish herself as a writer of renown, a literary force to be regarded seriously. They would lead her to a place no other African American poet or writer held.

A Street in Bronzeville was published in August 1945. It hit Afro-America with the force of an atomic bomb. But it was by no means destructive. It was life-affirming for black people, who often felt a strong need to prove they were equal to whites because many whites were so blatantly disproving of this essential fact. Gwendolyn was important because she surpassed not only the expectations of whites about black people but whites themselves.

The first poem in the collection is "the old-marrieds."

> But in the crowding darkness not a word did they say
> Though the pretty-coated bird had piped so lightly all the day.
> And he had seen the lovers in the little side-streets,
> And she had heard the morning stories clogged with sweets.

It was quite a time for loving. It was midnight. It was May.
But in the crowding darkness not a word did they say.

The speaker of the poem is omniscient, observing the absence of
intimacy in an intimate setting. The eye of the poet is penetrating,
as in a newsreel; the language pristine, almost mocking as the poem
begins.

Whether Gwendolyn's intention was to create a newsreel effect or
not, she begins her most public announcement of herself as a poet by
breaking with the past. This is neither a dialect nor sentimental poem; it
is neither blues-infused, as Hughes's work was, nor exotic. The characters
in the bed are not the stereotypically hypersexual Negroes of the white
imagination. They are sedate, mature, and sexually repressed. No one
had imagined Negroes in poetry in this way before. They were surpris-
ingly, refreshingly human. Indeed, Gwendolyn began with a surprising
imaginative and empathetic leap. She was a young poet, twenty-eight,
writing about middle-aged or elderly people. She was a relatively young
wife writing about a couple who had been married for decades.

The poem opens with the conjunction "but" as if to indicate that
the reader might be caught in a sentence that began a while ago. We are
engaged not only in that poem but in a volume of poems. Gwendolyn
suggests a street in Bronzeville with the phrase "crowding darkness";
she also suggests a claustrophobic darkness so close that it is intimate.
But the couple in the poem does not speak, and they are not inti-
mate in word or gesture. This disconnect is in spite of the romantic
events of the day that should have brought them closer together. Even
though it was the time for lovemaking, they do not make love. They
crowd like strangers in a crowd of darkness, as each of the residents
of Bronzeville may be a stranger in a dark crowd.

Gwendolyn continues the "Street in Bronzeville" section of the
volume with nineteen more portraits in verse exploring characters and
landmarks of the community. After "the old-marrieds" come two
popular masterpieces: "kitchenette building" and the aforementioned
"the mother." Wright had argued that "the mother" should not be

published in the book, and the poem is still controversial today because the subject is so controversial. Gwendolyn could not have been a more revolutionary black feminist in the writing of and steadfast inclusion of this poem in her inaugural volume.

These two poems have a great impact—the former in its understanding of the day-to-day stresses of "drylongso"—or everyday, ordinary black people—living in cut-up apartments with bathrooms separate from each unit, one bathroom per floor, five units sharing one bathroom; the latter in its understanding of the mother who has had an abortion (possibly more than one). There was no reliable birth control then beyond abstinence. Prophylactics were widespread, but unreliable. Abortion remains a hot-button topic today, even though it is legal. At the time the poem was written, though, abortions were illegal and dangerous, often performed in less than sterile conditions.

THE MOTHER

Abortions will not let you forget.
You remember the children you got that you did not get,
The damp small pulps with a little or with no hair,
The singers and workers that never handled the air.

The poem is a dramatic monologue. The speaker is a woman seized by guilt, anguish, and regret. The poem goes on in hypnotic effect offering a description of lives and people who might have been but will not. The poem is a plea for understanding of the mother's action, a plea from her to her children who she says she has deprived of many detailed aspects of life. Her only defense is this:

Believe me, I loved you all.
Believe me, I knew you, though faintly, and I loved, I loved you
All.

What is telling about the poem is that the narrator offers such a tender description of the lives not spent as she describes her crime.

She does not offer any justification or rationale because she herself cannot articulate one that is as forceful as their loss and her own. It is a remarkable poem that can serve as an argument for or against abortion. It simply is. Gwendolyn said that she herself had never had an abortion. She was artist enough to embody the pain of a woman who has had one.

It was not only artistic daring that distinguished Gwendolyn. There were few forums for black poets and writers in the late 1930s and 1940s. But the George Cleveland Hall Branch Library on Forty-Eighth and Michigan provided one such place. Initially, the librarian, Vivian Harsh, had concentrated on developing a vast collection of books and materials on Negro literature, life, and history. Then, in tune with Richard Wright's essay "Blueprint for Black Writing"—in which he encouraged a literature by Negroes truly reflective of the genuine humanity of Negroes, and the development of a readership for such a literature—Harsh opened the library as a forum for poets and writers. Initially organized in October 1933 as the Book Review and Forum, the library's "chief adult activity," its aim was to "enrich the lives of readers and draw attention to books by black writers."[1]

During those years, poets and writers who read at the Hall Branch Library included William Attaway, Arna Bontemps, Horace Cayton and St. Clair Drake (the coauthors of *Black Metropolis*), Langston Hughes, Zora Neale Hurston, Alain Locke, Margaret Walker, and Richard Wright—as well as Gwendolyn Brooks.[2] The Hall Branch Library was a national cultural beacon, and it was in its light that Gwendolyn was amplified in Chicago.

In the 1940s, Gwendolyn also read her poetry, accompanied by a harpist, at the South Side Community Art Center, whose director was her old friend Margaret Taylor Goss. These sophisticated afternoon salons showcasing Gwendolyn were warmly reviewed in the *Chicago Defender*.

Besides reading in the Hall Branch Library and South Side Community Art Center, Gwendolyn drew audiences elsewhere in the city when *A Street in Bronzeville* was released. She stepped out into a world that was somewhat prepared for her in its appetite for reading. But were they ready for her revolutionary vision?

In literature, Gwendolyn and other female Visionaries were not the only women who rose to the forefront during wartime. In 1944, schoolteachers Fern Gayden and Alice Browning founded *Negro Story* magazine to publish the work of Negro writers who represented Negroes as real human beings and not the stock characters usually found in print. Browning had been impelled by a rejection slip from *Esquire* magazine of one of her own stories and the idea of *Story* magazine.[3] She wanted a *Story* magazine for Negroes. Gayden had been a member of the South Side Writers Club with Richard Wright, and Browning was a dynamic woman whose penchant for organization lasted into her most-senior years. In the 1980s, she was still a vibrant, light-skinned lady with bright lipstick, a presence on the black Chicago literary scene as she organized an annual Black Writers Conference. It was always a well-attended event with national representation. Alice was energetic, smart, and young at heart, as committed to black literature as she had been in 1944.

During World War II, paper stock was hard to come by, so the two women purchased some from the *Chicago Defender*. They published the prominent and promising Negro writers: Richard Wright, Chester Himes, Ralph Ellison, poets Frank Marshall Davis, Margaret Walker, and, of course, Gwendolyn Brooks. The journal lasted from 1944 to 1946, and Gwendolyn gained additional notice through it. Readers of these national organs were waiting for the arrival of work by a poet of gathering recognition. *Negro Story* and the *Chicago Defender* heralded the publication of *A Street in Bronzeville*.

In their life as a young married couple, Gwendolyn and Henry lived in a number of residences in Bronzeville. Several of these were kitchenette buildings. Gwendolyn knew the sounds and odors of these spaces. She knew the preoccupations of its denizens, the mentality that circled round "rent" and "feeding a wife" in the male province or "satisfying a man" in the female province. These were quotidian and prevailing concerns. What was "a dream?" And how could it fare against the heavy necessities of reality itself?

KITCHENETTE BUILDING

We are things of dry hours and the involuntary plan,
Grayed in, and gray. "Dream" makes a giddy sound, not strong
Like "rent," "feeding a wife," "satisfying a man."

But could a dream send up through onion fumes
Its white and violet, fight with fried potatoes
And yesterday's garbage ripening in the hall,
Flutter, or sing an aria down these rooms

Even if we were willing to let it in,
Had time to warm it, keep it very clean,
Anticipate a message, let it begin?

We wonder. But not well! not for a minute!
Since Number Five is out of the bathroom now,
We think of lukewarm water, hope to get in it.

Life is grim in these kitchenette buildings. The color gray captures the mood of entrapment as in a prison. People here are not people; they are things, dehumanized by the nature of a system they did not volunteer for but were assigned to. To be strong is to meet the requirements of day-to-day living: pay rent, buy groceries, and satisfy a man's sexual needs (though not a woman's). A dream cannot withstand the weight of reality; reality stinks. A dream must be nurtured, takes a measure of attention. Do the residents have time for such a thing? They cannot even consider it long, for a realistic necessity comes up and they have to meet necessity. They take what they can get.

At first the poem seems to have an appealing comic ending, but upon reflection, it is sad. The best that one can hope for is lukewarm water for a bath.

The poems "the mother" and "kitchenette building" offer potent portraits of lives lived in desperation. They are elegantly executed and do not belabor the points Gwendolyn is making with these poor people. Other Bronzeville residents are memorable. Often quoted are "hunchback girl: she thinks of heaven," "a song in the front yard," "the preacher ruminates behind the sermon," "Sadie and Maud," "when you have forgotten Sunday: the love story," and "of DeWitt Williams on his way to Lincoln Cemetery."

"Sadie and Maud" and "a song in the front yard" share a theme of the satisfaction of the fast life and the deprivation of being safe and sheltered and good. And the couple in "when you have forgotten Sunday: the love story" manage to be actively sexual in a committed relationship. There is even a sweet excitement in the urgency of their love. In this poem, Gwendolyn endorses romantic sexual love. There is no child or children breaking the romantic mood. Perhaps these are young married people being celebrated. This couple and their circumstance come closest to Gwendolyn's own. The female lover has a "presentiment" that the war will be over before the male lover is called to service. In any case, the war is raging and the speaker may be addressing a beloved one absent because he is a soldier. We do not know, but we are engaged.

Gwendolyn, in her fashion, was an advocate for sexual liberation, the shrugging off of middle-class Puritanical values. Gwendolyn Brooks as a poet, that is. "Sadie and Maud" and "a song in the front yard" both witness the fulfillment that "combing life with a fine tooth" provided; explorations and adventures bring forth gifts to the spirit. Experience and wisdom were gathered. Children were the offspring of sexual exploration and openness. Spinsterhood and powerlessness, like a little brown mouse living in an old house, were the result of adhering to the expectations of others, following the rules.

Gwendolyn herself had broken ranks with her parents' authority. She married young. But in her personal life, she had not thumbed her nose at middle-class morality. Perhaps a part of her did yearn to live freely as did the speaker in "a song of the front yard"—wearing black stockings and strutting down the street with paint on her face.

Gwendolyn was the opposite of that image, demure and dignified. But she has more to say on the topic of female sexuality. Her "Queen of the Blues" is an ample, hip-shaking, shimmying singer who craves the respectability of a lady. She says, "Men are low down / Dirty and mean. / Why don't they tip / Their hats to a queen?" This queen pays the penalties of living outside the bounds of respectability, of singing and performing in a sexualized arena. This suggests that if Gwendolyn were not a full advocate for sexual exploration, at least she spoke bravely about the subject. It is as if Gwendolyn were dialoguing with herself on the benefits and detriments of sexual experience. For her, the argument is weighted in favor of sexual experience and passion. Young Gwendolyn was a gentlewoman and an artist, and her weighing in on the side of sexual expression was a call to love, experimentation, and the full living of life. She did not believe women should be closed in or fenced off from life. To explore female sexuality was to enter into an unspoken terrain. She entered this terrain throughout the volume.

Other residents of the Bronzeville street are represented in the remaining poems of the section. Gwendolyn's vision was radical in her selection of whom she saw and the way in which she saw them. She imagined a hunchback girl who dreamed of a straight heaven. This awareness of a Negro girl with a physical abnormality is highly unusual and is a testament to Gwendolyn's extended sensitivity to people. She imagined a preacher "ruminating behind a sermon" on the possible loneliness of God. This irreverent view of the Most High demonstrates Gwendolyn's social and religious daring. Church people might have been offended by the poem. Church people might also have been offended by a "living lady" who retreated from the sexual desires of suitors into a devout and living death of religiosity, only to be preyed upon by a lecherous preacher. There is an innocent accidental child murderer, an adulteress, and a boyfriend with "patent leather hair" on this street. DeWitt Williams was "a plain black boy" on his way to his burial, his body being carried past landmarks of his Bronzeville.

When Richard Wright served as Harper & Brothers' in-house reader for the volume, he suggested that Gwendolyn needed a long poem or several short poems that spoke in a "personal" way about her feelings for the residents of Bronzevillle. Gwendolyn responded to this call with one of her signature pieces, "The Sundays of Satin Legs Smith." It is a narrative of a day in the life of a Negro youth—a zoot-suiter. Gwendolyn would say about these sources of her inspiration, "You probably don't remember the zoot-suiters; they were still around in the forties, in the early forties. They were not only black men but Puerto Rican, too, who would wear these suits with the wide shoulders, and the pants did balloon out and then come down to tapering ends, and they wore chains—perhaps you've seen them in the movies. That's the kind of person I was writing about in 'The Sundays of Satin Legs Smith.'"[4] She refers to the zoot-suiters' hats "'like bright umbrellas' which implies that he is protecting himself under that fancy wideness." Gwendolyn explores the interior by scrupulously recording the exterior, and by intimately addressing the reader.

> Inamoratas, with an approbation,
> Bestowed his title. Blessed his inclination.

That is, a girlfriend, with a kiss, gave him the nickname that honored his walk and tendency to dress in satin-like fabrics.

Gwendolyn perfects the detached yet cozy tone of the newsreel in this extended narrative that strays from descriptive narrative in a few lines when she makes her social agenda most plain. She departs from her elaborate documentary overview and speaks directly to the reader in a most heartfelt way.

> People are so in need, in need of help.
> People want so much that they do not know.

These lines resonate and fairly ache off the page. Gwendolyn advocates directly for the poor, black, and dispossessed who suffer

"Promise piled over and betrayed" by the greed of unnamed others. She advocates for young men like Satin Legs, who spend their Sundays dressing up, going to the movies and out to eat with girlfriends they will enjoy sexually at the end of the evening. What else is there to do? Do they not deserve the better things of life? Do they not deserve to contribute to the world more than their style?

In the sixth stanza, Gwendolyn says that Satin Legs might have a chance at the finer things if there were done "a lot of equalizing things, / Remove a little ermine, say, from kings, / Shake hands with paupers and appoint them men." Gwendolyn suggests that we be still "unless we care to set the world a-boil." In other words, to even consider these ideas is dangerous.

Satin Legs Smith spends an inordinate amount of time at his toilette, inspecting his closet full of "wonder-suits" in very loud colors with padded shoulders and wide-legged pants. He dresses, "dances down" the dirty steps of the hotel where he lives, eats a light continental breakfast, joins the chaos of the neighborhood, the sounds melding around him. He is oblivious to the sights of the environment and poor Negro people. He stops and blues songs rise. Gwendolyn counterpoints that he does not hear the European classics, the suggestion being that they are inherently better. Satin Legs could not relate to this music. It does not relate to the occurrences of his life.

The pasts of his ancestors lean against
Him. Crowd him. Fog out his identity.
Hundreds of hungers mingle with his own,

Critic Edward Bland had convinced Gwendolyn and Henry that Negroes live in a pre-individual state with identities framed only as part of the collective. Here, Gwendolyn has Satin Legs Smith merge as one with his ancestors in a pre-individualistic state, but even more so, she suggests a racial identity akin to that expressed by Margaret Walker in her 1942 poem "For My People." But Satin Legs rejects the voices of the past and accepts his vacant present.

Judges he walks most powerfully alone,
That everything is—simply what it is.

At the movies he acts out and boos the kissing Caucasians, especially the white woman, who is forbidden fruit. He is permitted to enjoy the asexual Mickey Mouse. He takes his lady "to dinner at Joe's Eats." The dates change, but she is always a woman of a certain type. She is a fast woman in too-high heels, with too-long nails, too much lipstick, veiled hat. He does not know any better about the kind of woman to choose for a lasting relationship, and he does not care to know, Gwendolyn assures us. They eat soul food and are full.

The poem concludes in italics, leaving nothing to the imagination, or everything to the imagination. Its tone is no longer detached.

Her body is like new brown bread
Under the Woolworth mignonette.
Her body is a honey bowl
Whose waiting honey is deep and hot
Her body is like summer earth,
Receptive, soft, and absolute . . .

The lines are sensual and earthy. The sex act is from a male perspective and so is the woman. The lines suggest a rich, sexual experience. But the last word, "absolute," suggests more. "Absolute," according to Merriam-Webster's dictionary, means (1) free from imperfection or mixture, (2) free from control, restriction, or qualification, (4) positive, (6) fundamental, ultimate. In the context of the poem, and in Satin Legs Smith's life, her body as representative of the sex act is the place or moment in which Satin Legs is free, positive, most fully realized. Everything in this long day has led us to this moment of freedom. Gwendolyn has done more than document the Sundays of Satin Legs Smith, the day in which he does not have to go to work. She has liberated him in art. She has done more than what Richard Wright has asked. She has surpassed his expectation and ability to explore, to a certain extent, the dispossessed.

In his September 1, 1945, column in the *Chicago Defender* following the publication of *A Street in Bronzeville*, Langston Hughes gave a strong endorsement of the book, praising all but one poem. He described "Ballad of Pearl May Lee" as "a kind of female Negro national anthem for all colored ladies who feel as bitterly about miscegenation as do Bilbo and Rankin." US senator Theodore Bilbo and Congressman John Rankin were two notorious white racist segregationists.

Hughes called "Ballad of Pearl May Lee" a "high colored [very dark skinned] Negro poem" from "a sharp and dramatic book of poems by a zooming, new talent on our literary horizons. . . . In her ballad in black and white in her book, brown-skin Gwendolyn Brooks of Chicago's dark South Side has wrapped in verse all her resentment and bitterness concerning the black man who seeks and finds a white sweet heart."

> *But you paid for your white arms. Sammy boy,*
> *And you didn't pay with money.*
> *You paid with your hide and my heart, Sammy boy,*
> *For your taste of pink and white honey,*

It may be true that "Hell hath no fury as a woman scorned," but it is also true in this case that grief can be hysterical. People seized by sudden mourning can erupt with powerful emotions. Pearl May Lee was a woman torn up by a desperate loss that she believed could have been avoided if her love had been returned. Alas, her beloved was enthralled by white women or light-skinned Negro women, and he was hanged for his lust for white women, the forbidden fruit of the South at that time. There is a thin line between love and hate; Pearl May Lee was seized by a rage that overwhelmed sorrow.

"Ballad of Pearl May Lee" is more complicated than Langston Hughes would have us believe. It begins with a Negro man being carted off to jail, while the Negro woman "cut her lungs with her laughter." This is painful laughter. By the next stanza, Pearl May Lee pictures the black beloved in a rat-infested cell, while she confesses there is no one more forlorn than she is. For all her laughter, Pearl May Lee is suffering emotionally.

The ballad continues to tell the story of Sammy Boy and how he paid for his taste of white milk with his life and Pearl May Lee's heart. Sammy and Pearl have had a sexual relationship in spite of the fact that he always had "bright skins on the brain." He used Pearl to fulfill his desires. She, on the other hand, loved him. Sammy Boy was lured by a white "vixen." His knees went weak. They had sex in the white girl's Buick. Flooded with shame after the act, the white girl cried rape, as often happened in the South. Sammy Boy was lynched, and Pearl May Lee was thrown into emotional chaos.

After Hughes's column appeared, there followed a dialogue about interracial dating and marriage in the *Chicago Defender*. Hughes had brought controversy to Gwendolyn and additional national attention. But controversy sells books. He proved that Gwendolyn would give people something to talk about. Gwendolyn, for her part, addressed two long-standing concerns in the poem—lynching and colorism. She had marched against lynching with the NAACP Youth Council, and she had felt the sting of colorism since childhood. She broadened her concerns as well, opening the door to address the issue of forbidden fruit and the lure of white women, as well as false claims of rape. The lure of white women would be a subject that black women poets of the 1960s would take up. Gwendolyn Brooks was a forerunner.

The name Doris "Dorie" Miller was legend among Negroes during World War II. He was highly regarded by whites, too. During the surprise attack on Pearl Harbor on December 7, 1941, in the dawn's light, Miller was below deck in the mess where Negroes were assigned to work in the segregated US Navy. He had just finished his duties as a cook and doing laundry for officers when the Japanese bombers began attacking the fleet and the alarm was sounded. Miller helped move his wounded captain to safety and then helped load two machine guns, firing at Japanese bombers. This was against regulations, as blacks were not supposed to fight in the Navy. Miller was next ordered to bring wounded soldiers to safety, which he did with no thought for his own safety and saved many lives. Eventually, the battleship *West Virginia* sank and all hands had to abandon ship.

Thus the stuff of legends is made. Gwendolyn Brooks captured the man and his actions in her classic persona poem "Negro Hero."

I had to kick their law into their teeth to save them.

Of course, the poem's speaker is addressing the fact that he had to courageously go against naval regulations in order to man a gun to shoot down the planes that delivered destruction and death to Americans, and he had to go against regulations by saving sailors when he was deemed worthy only to cook and clean.

Gwendolyn continues, making another one of her astonishing imaginative and empathetic leaps, speaking in the voice of the young black male sailor.

I loved. And a man will guard when he loves.
Their white-gowned democracy was my fair lady
With her knife lying cold, straight, in the softness of her sweet-flowing
sleeve.

Thus, in this war-torn poem, Gwendolyn grasped the heart of the Negro dilemma: an aching patriotism and a love of liberty and equality that is betrayed. The poem's dedication reads "to suggest Dorie Miller," for the poem is not solely about Miller. It is about all black soldiers and sailors and citizens who believed in and gave of themselves for the dream of America.

Gwendolyn Brooks had a love affair with black Chicago. Certain landmarks make *A Street in Bronzeville* a quintessentially Chicago book: Lincoln Cemetery, the Lower West Side, the Rhumboogie, Brass Rail, Keyhole, DeLisa, and Cabin Inn, down on Calumet, Forty-Seventh

Street, underneath the "L," the Northwest Corner, Prairie, the Warwick and Savoy dance halls, Lafayette Street. Gwendolyn lays claim to the space and sinks the roots of her poems in so deep that they grow up organically out of the experience of the Black Metropolis. Readers of the volume hear the echoes of inhabitants and their footsteps on the designated spaces.

Certain parts of the closing sonnet sequence are exquisite; all are deeply moving. The sonnet "Gay Chaps at the Bar" is superb. "Gay," of course, at that time, meant happy or merry. And the bar is where drinks are served, or might it be another bar that the patrons faced—one of color, reality? We enter the mysteries of the experiences of men at war, particularly black men at war. In language edging us deeper, Gwendolyn recreates the tumult and urgency of young black men in harm's way, including by fellow soldiers, since black troops were known to have been killed by white soldiers in boot camps stateside. The sonnet sequence is dedicated in part to Gwendolyn's brother, "Sgt. Raymond Brooks and all soldiers."

The sequence also serves as a potent argument against war, each sonnet detailing a different aspect of the experience of serving one's country in the military during wartime. "Gay Chaps at the Bar" was first published in *Poetry* magazine, which awarded the poem its prestigious prize at the Writers Conference at Northwestern University.

The first sonnet opens with an epigram from a letter from Lieutenant William Couch in the South Pacific,

> *. . . and guys I knew in the States, young officers, return from the front crying and trembling. Gay chaps at the bar in Los Angeles, Chicago, New York. . .*

The poem recounts the bravado expressed by the newly minted officers on leave before war—how they drank, caroused, and courted women. They knew how to talk like white men, to give a woman a certain look. But they did not know how to separate their inner selves from the blood and guts of war; did not know how to be casual about seeing their comrades die or face the possibility of their own deaths.

They had neither inner nor patriotic band music sufficient to drown out the roar of machine guns, rifles, and cannons. Nothing prepared them for or countered the horrible reality of war. That is the gist of the poem, but the hurt and anguish are in the tightly contained music of the off-rhyme sonnet.

Gwendolyn called this sequence of sonnets "a souvenir," something that her brother and others who had served could keep. She downplayed the value of what she had given because nothing could compare to them offering their lives.

These poems journey through individual identities, ghosts of fallen comrades, the futility of racism, to agnosticism. The final poem, "the progress," suggests that there is no progress, for another war will come: "Listen, listen. The step / Of iron feet again. And again wild." Gwendolyn's position on war itself is clear: she is opposed to it. But she also suggests that it is inevitable.

A Street in Bronzeville was given an excellent review in the *Chicago Tribune*: "Chicago Can Take Pride in New, Young Voice in Poetry." The volume was reviewed by Paul Engle, who had served as poetry judge of the Midwestern Writers Conference and presented Gwendolyn her award. Engle took care to note that *A Street in Bronzeville* would be important no matter the color of its author. "Her poems would be finely lyrical and delightfully witty without the fact of color ever being mentioned," he wrote. "This is a remarkable thing which must be praised. . . . They are handsome and real and genuine poems by a civilized American citizen. . . . This [poetry] is the real thing. So is Miss Brooks."[5] It is rather easy to see the backhanded compliment in being called a "civilized American citizen." Why would she be assumed otherwise? Even kindness toward Negroes hid condescension.

Still, even after a reporter from the *Chicago Defender* came to do a full-page feature on Gwendolyn upon the publication of *A Street in Bronzeville*, when the journalist left, the Blakelys remained in their cramped newspaper- and book-stacked unit. People of five kitchenette units still shared one bathroom. Housing was a depressing issue and caused tension in Gwendolyn and Henry's marriage.

CHAPTER FOUR

Hitting Her Stride

Gwendolyn entered a new period of endeavors, reviewing books for the *Chicago Tribune* and *Chicago Sun-Times*. Later, she would review for *Negro Digest*, which brought in necessary additional income for the family. Henry worked, giving estimates on auto repair jobs for an auto shop in which he was a partner, but he also held jobs as a mechanic, factory worker, and truck driver at various times.

Gwendolyn continued to engage in her literary work around the performance of her life as a devoted mother and homemaker. That was unchanged. Her poetry, however, was venturing out in two directions. The first was a series of poems, "American Family Brown." This was rejected by Harper & Brothers in 1947.[1] Later it would be resurrected and revised into the remarkable nontraditional novel *Maud Martha*, which I will discuss in the pages that follow.

The second direction, more immediately fruitful, was in the creation of the collection *Annie Allen*, which had begun as "Hester Allen." Years after its publication, Gwendolyn said, "I thought of 'The Iliad' and said, 'I'll call this 'The Anniad.' At first, interestingly enough, I called her Hester Allen, and I wanted then to say 'The Hesteriad,' but I forgot why I changed it to Annie. . . . I was fascinated by what words might do there in the poem. You can tell that it's labored, a poem that's very interested in the mysteries and magic of technique."[2]

Annie Allen is studied but it is also a great technical achievement, for Gwendolyn was interested in this aspect of her art. She was also interested in appeasing her Harper & Brothers editor, Elizabeth Lawrence, who had encouraged her to pursue poems that were more "universal," that is to say, less blatantly about the African American experience. That was the agenda of *Annie Allen.* These efforts were rewarded.

Initially, the first poems of what was then called *Hester Allen* received mixed reviews among the staff at Harper, so Lawrence sent the poems to be read by the poet Genevieve Taggard, whose response was eight hand-written pages of non-support. She found the poems by turns "monotonous," "obscure," "imitative," and "a good exercise," but not "a work of art for the reader."[3] Lawrence sent the review to Gwendolyn with a note to soften the blows of the negative response. But she stood by Taggard's response and closed her own letter, "But for the moment you often put a burden on the reader that is not commensurate with the rewards. You are too good a poet to have to resort to trick and shock devices."[4]

Yet Lawrence was excited about some poems in the collection and sent Gwendolyn a contract with a hundred-dollar advance, half of what she had received for *A Street in Bronzeville.* Perhaps it was a half-hearted show of support from her publisher, but it was something. And the volume would see the light of day. That was the important thing. Gwendolyn changed the collection's name to *Annie Allen,* wrote new poems, deleted some old ones, and revised others. She mailed the completed manuscript to her editor on January 14, 1949.[5]

It appears that Gwendolyn had to do a lot to stay in print. Harper & Brothers had not guaranteed her publication of her next book of poetry. They had rejected the "American Family Brown" collection and given a lukewarm response to *Annie Allen.* After Gwendolyn submitted her completed manuscript for *Annie Allen,* there were still editorial notes to contend with, wherein Lawrence attempted to dissuade Gwendolyn from gems, two excellent poems that were critical of white people. For the poems "downtown vaudeville" and "I love those little booths at Bevenuti's," Gwendolyn had to clarify her authorial intentions. She did take Lawrence's advice on deletions from another poem, but the point is, Gwendolyn Brooks, even as a so-called literary darling, met resistance and had to push back. She did not do this with arrogance or verbal aggression. She persuaded, negotiated her way as "a light, and diplomatic bird," as she described in a poem in *Annie Allen*. She made her way with diplomacy, forthrightness, and gentility, skills she had honed while serving as publicity and press person for the Chicago youth council of the NAACP.

Annie Allen is a more seemingly personal book than *A Street in Bronzeville*. It opens with eleven loosely connected poems about the character of Annie Allen or ruminations from her. Gwendolyn breaks with the people-scape of *A Street in Bronzeville* to engage the interiors of subjects and ideas, while dealing with exteriors in a different way.

Annie Allen is very much a geography of the mind and heart. It begins with "the birth in the narrow room." The title alone tells the circumstance of the child's birth; "a narrow room" is pressed in on by prevailing oppressions that Gwendolyn would not or could not then name but which existed—racism, colorism, classicism, and sexism. The baby is described as "Blurred and stupendous," meaning this child is stained or colored and of a size that made people gasp. In the poem, Gwendolyn attends her own birth, foreshadowing her own stature. In a literal sense, this child is a big, colored baby. Let us be completely candid, however. The first line of the poem is "Weeps out of western country something new"—not a happy omen. One thinks of Countee Cullen's agonized yet affirming words from 1927, "We were not made eternally to weep." This child of Gwendolyn's poem is aware of her cramped circumstances, but rejects them as she "prances nevertheless with gods and fairies." The child finds freedom in imagination, just as Gwendolyn had.

She needs her imagination, too, for at the heart of the poem she is aware of the strictures placed upon her. "How pinchy is my room! how can I breathe!" Eerily, these words call to mind the "I can't breathe!" cry of Eric Garner and the Black Lives Matter movement.

This young movement and generation need the force of imagination to thrive, to gain breathing space. Gwendolyn Brooks is ever the foremother.

The artistic achievement of *Annie Allen* was hailed by Richard Wright in Paris, Langston Hughes in the *Chicago Defender*, J. Saunders Redding in *Phylon*. In the *Defender*, Gertrude Martin described much of the work as "studied" but endorsed its merit. "The Anniad," for example, requires study to understand it (if one ever really does). It is the center of the volume but is a cerebral adventure, allegorical and modern at once, and difficult to fully grasp.

Gwendolyn Brooks was extremely well-read in the classics, evidenced by her reference to the "higher gods," the Titans, and the "lesser gods," the gods of Mount Olympus, possibly. In "The Anniad," the title character, Annie, goes through a period of fascination with classical writers and characters—Plato, Aeschylus, Seneca, Mimnermus, Pliny, Dionysus—and of course, the title, "The Anniad," is a clever play on "The Iliad."

"The Anniad" could be a symbolic treatment of a romance and of a woman's evolution into maturity, but Gwendolyn grounds it substantially in the reality of World War II and the postwar lives of its principals. It is too realistic to be simple allegory. The veteran, Annie's lover, suffers from post-traumatic stress syndrome. He is a "man of tan." She knelt before him.

"The Anniad" also moves like a film, firmly grounded in the reality of its main characters, richly portraying the coming of age of a young Negro woman named Annie. We meet her thusly:

> *Think of sweet and chocolate,*
> *Left to folly or to fate,*
> *Whom the higher gods forgot,*
> *Whom the lower gods berate;*
> *Physical and underfed*
> *Fancying on the feather bed*
> *What was never and is not*

A scene is set. But our heroine is not a usual one. She is a dark-skinned girl. She is aware and we are aware that she suffers because of her skin color. The higher gods, omniscient and omnipotent, know of her but do nothing to make her dreams come true. The lower gods, who serve as overseers and maybe white racists or Negro colorists, lord it over the sweet, chocolate heroine. Gwendolyn does not belabor the point about Annie being powerless and abused by fates and fortunes and those who exact these. She makes her point and moves on.

The diction of *Annie Allen*, especially in "The Anniad," is elevated and decidedly noncolloquial. Gwendolyn chooses language that offers entrance to the classical European tradition—language that proves that a black woman who is a poet can be as difficult as T. S. Eliot. She is capable of manipulating language and wresting meanings out of it. At the same time that her choice of elevated, even obscure, language suggests the elevated nature of her subjects, she argues through her choice of diction for the dignity of Negro people, worthy of being regarded as equals to any white people. The story she tells is worthy of most serious consideration. With its subtexts of equality and "universality," it is an argument for integration, the prevailing goal for Gwendolyn and her generation of African Americans.

And there was cause for optimistic belief in coming equality and integration. In 1948, the restrictive covenants of white property owners seeking to forbid the ownership of property by blacks in certain areas were struck down as unenforceable by the Supreme Court. Thus Negroes were free to move into areas that previously had been closed to them. And move they did.

It is in this context of optimism mixed with postwar trauma that the majority of "The Anniad" takes place. But the poem begins in a time before the war. As noted, Annie was daydreaming on a feather bed. She is imagining the arrival of a heroic lover who will sweep her away. This man is the beau ideal. Annie makes herself up and combs her kinky hair that fights the comb. A tan suitor comes calling but takes things slowly. Then the thin master, a man with an arrogantly masculine style, takes over, and she lapses into a submissive female role. She adores the thin master. He puts her "in his pocket," captures her completely. She genuflects to him as if he were a deity.

Then her deity is drafted and goes to war. Annie is driven to distraction by worry. He comes home, nervous and feeling out of place. He finds it difficult to adjust to civilian life. He seeks relief from his anxiety, but he does not want the relief that Annie offers. He wants a loud, gorgeous blonde (or light-skinned) woman, a hip-talking woman. He finds a vulgar "maple banshee." They lose themselves in sex and alcohol.

Meanwhile, Annie is missing a justice of the peace, wedding vows, a honeymoon, any symbol of a union. She seeks solace in the changing of the seasons: winter snow, spring greens, summer heat, and its loneliness. November suits her best with its richly falling leaves. She turns to reading the classics but finds her books insufficient. She wakes from her desperate efforts to forget. She curses her lover, but she accepts his return. Or does she? At poem's end, Annie is mature at twenty-four and left with a faint dream and the remembered embrace of a love: "Hugging old and Sunday sun / kissing in her kitchenette / The minuets of memory." She has experienced the ardor of young love, disappointment, and endured a compromise with the reality of life.

This summary of "The Anniad" does not convey the overwhelming artistry of the piece. Its vocabulary both traditional and inventive, its myriad connotations, its many metaphors combine to create an experience that is at once filmic—deeply visual, visceral—and a kind of immersion.

The ever ingenious and revolutionary Gwendolyn continues to invent new poetic forms with "the sonnet-ballad," fourteen lines of a song-story of a young woman lamenting her lover killed in battle. She watches him marching off to war and knows he will not return. The poem is a ballad in its narrative and rhythms. Of it, Gwendolyn said, "Its one claim to fame is that I invented it." Perhaps Gwendolyn is too modest here, for the form is engaging in its alluring rhythm, and the poem's compelling story is tightly contained and fulfilled.

"The Womanhood," the section that concludes *Annie Allen*, consists of twenty-one poems. Gwendolyn continued to energize the sonnet form with the first poems of "The Womanhood," including poem 2 of section I, "the children of the poor." Just as she had revivified the sonnet in the soldier poems of *A Street in Bronzeville*, she breathed life and new commentary into the soliloquy sonnet "the children of the poor," spotlighting not just race but economic class in language that was not veiled.

2.
What shall I give my children? who are poor,
Who are adjudged the leastwise of the land,
Who are my sweetest lepers, who demand
No velvet and no velvety velour;

Gwendolyn addresses racial segregation, which was very much a part of official US policy in certain areas and unofficially in others at the time she was writing. These "sweetest lepers" do not demand much. They do not demand the trappings of wealth, "velvet" and "velvety velour." The "children of the poor" do not ask for economic justice. They ask to be seen as human.

And when they were not, Gwendolyn advocated brave action.

FIRST FIGHT, THEN FIDDLE
First fight. Then fiddle. Ply the slipping string
With feathery sorcery; muzzle the note
With hurting love . . .

Win war. Rise bloody, maybe not too late
For having first to civilize a space
Wherein to play your violin with grace.

Sonnet 4 might first be taken as a World War II poem, exhorting soldiers to do battle and reclaim the world for democratic ideals. But upon consideration, the new integration afforded by the dismissal of restrictive covenants may be the background for this poem. It exhorts optimistic African Americans to venture forth bravely to previously white neighborhoods and inhabit property in which they might prosper. Gwendolyn would deal more directly with this concept of fighting to "civilize a space" in a later poem, when the issue heated up in real time.

In sections 2 and 3 of "the children of the poor," Gwendolyn deals specifically with incidents from the childhood of Hank, her precocious and curious son. "His lesions are legion. / But reaching is his rule." He may have scrapes and scars, but he continues to explore his environment. In a humorous turn, He appears disguised as a "light-eyed girl" who buries a dead pigeon. These two poems give glimpses into Gwendolyn's nature as a mother, at once tender and affectionate.

But she is also a working mother, and section 4 treats her attempt to negotiate a way of being in the world. She studies "a light and diplomatic bird" so that she might learn evasiveness and necessary tact when dealing with powerful others. One feels the inner workings of Gwendolyn's sense of herself at war, hoping for a happy resolution, "make miniature / Valhalla of my heart." Valhalla, a mythic heaven for warriors, is where Gwendolyn saw herself.

One of the few false notes that she makes as a poet is section 5's "old laughter," in which she speaks of Africa positively if inaccurately, considering it as a romantic, idyllic land of laughter and spices. This is in sharp contrast to her early predecessor Phillis Wheatley, who saw the ancestral home as a "benighted soul."

Gwendolyn acknowledges that once Africa was a joyous place, when its people were free of kidnapping and chattel slavery. There is a kernel of truth in what she is saying. And there is an attempt, in the poem, to grapple with, though fleetingly, the legacy and ravages of slavery and colonization. The poem was written when Gwendolyn was a teenager, and she was not ready to address these issues fully at this point in her maturity. She did not have the information to bring her acute insight to bear on the subject. What is important is that the poem's positivity suggests her identification with Africa, which would develop as time brought clarity.

Section 6, "the rites for Cousin Vit," is a vivid portrait of a recently deceased woman who was so vital in life that it seems she cannot be gone, that she is ever reliving her life. Cousin Vit goes to bars, "love rooms," spills bad wine, and dances "snake hips." Unladylike, she walks alone in parks and alleys. She leads an adventuresome life, gaining by chance some happiness or sometimes experiencing fits of laughter or crying. The last word of the poem is simply a one-word sentence, "Is." Cousin Vit exists and lives always in the present tense. Such a woman who broke the rules lives life on her own terms and can never be consigned to simple memory. She can never be consigned to death. She is life itself. Thus, Gwendolyn salutes the feminine principle—the life force exemplified by one woman.

Of section 7, "I love those little booths at Benvenuti's," Gwendolyn's editor at Harper & Brothers, Elizabeth Lawrence, had said it was simply "reportorial." Gwendolyn responded that she meant it to be "poetically reportorial," and there is much inside the report.[6] White people go to Benvenuti's to spy on the citizens of Bronzeville, to be entertained by the local color. The white people are disappointed because the colored people do not perform in anticipated, colorful ways. Negroes simply eat in a civilized manner, laugh quietly, and leave the place with the white people in it. Gwendolyn makes two points: one, white people could enter black neighborhoods unharmed, and two, Negroes were just like everyone else.

Gwendolyn takes the opposite approach in section 8, "Beverly Hills, Chicago." Henry and Gwendolyn would drive through the posh neighborhood and dream of a dream house. Invariably the neighborhood of fine homes and well-tended lawns was a white one. In this poem, African Americans drive through such a neighborhood to see how the wealthy live. The poem's epigram is "and the people live till they have white hair," from a poem by E. M. Price. Brooks's poem has a universal appeal for those who have not, for it is customary for people of limited means to cruise through affluent neighborhoods and fantasize about the houses there and the lives lived seemingly without want. In "Beverly Hills, Chicago," Gwendolyn cruises through the minds of the seekers and speaks what is there. The speaker recognizes that the rich suffer and die. It is a sad poem without the bitterness of envy.

> *Nobody is furious. Nobody hates these people.*
> *. . .*
> *We do not want them to have less.*
> *But it is only natural that we should think we have not enough.*
> *We drive on, we drive on.*
> *When we speak to each other our voices are a little gruff.*

But there is a touch of anger at the injustice of the world that gives so much to some and so little to them, driving by. Gwendolyn hedges her anger when she writes, "It is only natural, however, that it should occur to us," as if to say "What we think is not the case." Gwendolyn does not openly embrace the idea of economic injustice. Is this the awareness of economic disparity the "truth" that Gwendolyn worries may come? Will the fact that many are deprived while a few prosper be a fact as bright as the sun and as hot? She of course addressed this in her work.

> TRUTH
> *And if sun comes*
> *How shall we greet him?*
> *Shall we not dread him,*
> *Shall we not fear him*
> *After so lengthy a*
> *Session with shade?*
>
> *Though we have wept for him,*
> *Though we have prayed*

All through the night-years—
What if we wake one shimmering morning to
Hear the fierce hammering
Of his firm knuckles
Hard on the door?

Shall we not shudder?—
Shall we not flee
Into the shelter, the dear thick shelter
Of the familiar
Propitious haze?

Sweet is it, sweet is it
To sleep in the coolness
Of snug unawareness.

The dark hangs heavily
Over the eyes.

Again, the concept of human indecisiveness in the face of facts may be about economic justice or simply a new awareness of any reality that had previously been hidden. People are not always willing to be awakened. This is an important concept, for it speaks to the nature and importance of bravery. We must be brave enough to face the truth, to welcome it, or we sleep forever, missing out on possibilities and the fullness of the present. We must be brave in order to engage our world and change it if we must. The poem is of singular importance. Written in the diplomatic language of its time, it could not speak directly to any one issue. It speaks universally to the importance of embracing the truth and ourselves.

An unpopular truth among African Americans is colorism. The assignment of worth based upon skin color and grade of hair is akin to racism, but it occurs inside the culture of people of color. Gwendolyn addressed it head-on.

STAND OFF, DAUGHTER OF THE DUSK

3
Stand off, daughter of the dusk,
And do not wince when the bronzy lads
Hurry to cream-yellow shining.
It is plausible. The sun is a lode.

True, there is silver under
The veils of the darkness.
But few care to dig in the night
For the possible treasure of stars.

Critic J. Saunders Redding objected to the poem on the grounds that it was too specific to African Americans and that whites would not understand. Perhaps Redding feared Gwendolyn was airing dirty laundry in public. As a rule, black women find the poem important as a sensitive treatment of a sensitive subject. It speaks to a truth that sprang from Gwendolyn's childhood—rejection based on skin color by people of color—and it was a favorite poem of Gertrude Martin, who wrote about it in the *Chicago Defender*.

Toward the end of "The Womanhood" and the volume *Annie Allen* are two reflections on race relations in America. The fourteenth poem examines African Americans who do not show enough backbone, who protest but without any fury. Rather, they beseech. "And he will follow many a cloven feet," writes Gwendolyn. The Negro who beseeches will be led by a devil or scoundrels. The eleventh poem, on the other hand, begins by looking at whites who have a difficult time accepting difference and must grudgingly admit that black people are human and therefore capable of injury.

Men of careful turns, haters of forks in the road,
The strain in the eye, that puzzlement, that owe—
Grant that I am human, that I hurt
That I can cry.

Now that black people have been admitted into society, they are told that the cruelties of the present are better than those of slavery time. The whites, according to Gwendolyn, say that prejudice is natural and appropriate.

> *Rise.*
> *Let us combine. There are no magics or elves*
> *Or timely godmothers to guide us. We are lost, must*
> *Wizard a track through our own screaming weed.*

The exhortation is clear: blacks must join forces with willing whites. They must press forward in a new way, for there is no historical precedent that she knows of to show them how to move forward through what lies ahead.

There Gwendolyn ends the adventure of *Annie Allen*, on a hearty, adult note. The romances of adolescence are done with. Her generation has been to war and back. They have birthed children who must be nurtured and guided. Restrictive covenants have been struck down. They have to fashion a new place and way in the modern world. And Gwendolyn is speaking for herself and all Negro Americans.

Upon the publication of *Annie Allen*, more than five hundred people came to the International House of the University of Chicago to celebrate the poet of Bronzeville at a book party. Gwendolyn was introduced by her "friend, mentor, president of the Midwestern Writers Conference," Mrs. Alice Manning Dickey. Gwendolyn's old friend Margaret Taylor Goss was the mistress of ceremonies. Also present were two pianists and the writers Era Bell Thompson, Metz T. P. Lockard, Henry Rago, and Jack Conroy. The large size of the audience was a testament to the chord that Gwendolyn had struck with her community with *A Street in Bronzeville*. She was celebrated in the press and with a radio play, *Poet in Bronzeville*, by Richard Durham. Gwendolyn also read her poetry over the radio and touched even more lives.

That fall, in 1949, Gwendolyn read her poetry at Howard University in Washington, DC, the apex of Negro education. She was well received by an institution that was hard to impress. Inez Stark, who had married and was now Inez Stark Boulton, lived nearby. Gwendolyn stayed with her for four days. Inez reported to Karl Shapiro, a white poet, that Gwendolyn's attitude to her "white friends and friends of white friends" was "free of any race's taint." Gwendolyn, she found, was fit for Shapiro's association.[7] Inez, who had once been a rebel, was now the self-appointed racial judge. When she and Gwendolyn went to New York together, Gwendolyn was not permitted to even leave her luggage at Inez's hotel for a short time. Inez did not protest. Gwendolyn was not naïve and got the picture.

Gwendolyn had to improvise a life in letters. She enjoyed the fruits of a certain success—a Guggenheim fellowship and publication in *Poetry* magazine, as well as two well-received volumes of poetry by a major publisher. But she was grounded in the reality of her life as a Negro woman. She and her husband did not have much money and lived in a cramped, book-filled space. She would add to those books more bearing her name.

CHAPTER FIVE

A Pulitzer Is a Smile

She and her son, Hank, then nine years old, had been on their way to the movies, just to get out of the house.

"The day I won the Pulitzer Prize was very exciting for me," Gwendolyn said. "My husband and I were having financial problems. And the lights were out. . . . A columnist from the *Sun-Times* called. 'Do you know that you've won the Pulitzer Prize?' . . . I felt at once different and the same."

Gwendolyn still took Hank to the movies. On the way, she wondered how she appeared to others. She wondered if she looked the same. One woman knew somehow. "Are you Gwendolyn Brooks?" she asked. "Didn't you win the Pulitzer Prize?" Gwendolyn did not know how the woman could have known as the award had not been announced officially. It was May 1, 1950.[1]

Gwendolyn's success was instantaneously applauded. The immediate post-Pulitzer period was a whirlwind of congratulations and praise that came by phone, letter, telegram. She was asked to do interviews, readings, and lectures on race relations. She accepted the readings, though she had never been comfortable speaking publicly, but declined lecturing on race relations. She still expressed her fullness in writing. The day after the announcement, she sent a telegram to

Elizabeth Lawrence, her editor at Harper & Brothers, saying, "Am sick with happiness and know how glad you are for me." Lawrence sent her flowers, and again Gwendolyn wrote expressing her gratitude: "The card made me want to cry. I have been wanting for years to make you proud. Because always you have gone out of your way to help me and to please me."[2]

Many years later, Gwendolyn would write of the Pulitzer, "It is a smile."[3] At worst she was being disingenuous; at best, ironic or profoundly understated. Being the first black person to be awarded a Pulitzer Prize in any genre placed Gwendolyn in the front ranks of Negro achievement. Her poetry was read by other great poets, such as T. S. Eliot. She was asked to be a judge for the National Book Award. In January 1951, the *Chicago Defender* listed her in a group of outstanding African Americans of achievement with Ralph Bunche, Nobel Peace Prize winner; Thurgood Marshall, NAACP special counsel; Jackie Robinson, the first African American to play in Major League Baseball; and Althea Gibson, who broke the color barrier in tennis. Gwendolyn was a success, a phenomenon. Her achievement placed her in the position of foremother to all other blacks who achieved literary success. Henceforth, when her name appeared in print, it would, more often than not, be preceded by "Pulitzer Prize–winning poet."

Gwendolyn's achievement had not been heralded with unanimous approval, however. On May 13, 1950, the *Saturday Review* took a survey of editors' choices for the prize. Most selected old favorites Robert Frost and William Carlos Williams. Gwendolyn was noted as "a writer of promise." But that was after she had won the Pulitzer Prize.

Gwendolyn gave a significant reading at the thirty-fifth annual convention of the Association for the Study of Negro Life and History, on October 28, 1950, in Atlanta. It was Gwendolyn and Henry's first trip to the Deep South. The keynote speaker was the inestimable Mary McLeod Bethune, educator, founder of Bethune-Cookman College and of the National Council of Negro Women, friend to Eleanor Roosevelt, and advisor to President Franklin Delano Roosevelt on the Federal Council of Negro Affairs.

Sitting beside her on the dais, Gwendolyn initially received a chilly reception from the esteemed Mrs. Bethune, though Gwendolyn was unusually chatty. Then Gwendolyn rose to read. She did not attempt to impress anyone by speaking extemporaneously. She simply read a selection of her poems, for her Aunt Beulah had once advised her that "poets poet." Gwendolyn was known to be an excellent reader of her own works. When Gwendolyn had finished reading, Mrs. Bethune turned to her and regarded her with warmth and admiration. They even posed for pictures together.[4]

Nineteen months after the Pulitzer announcement, Gwendolyn gave birth to a daughter, Nora, on September 8, 1951. Nora's birth limited the poet's ability to travel. Gwendolyn was scheduled to participate in a literary festival at Jackson College in Mississippi in November 1952, along with Langston Hughes; Margaret Walker, who taught there; Owen Dodson of Howard University; Melvin Tolson; and Mary Elizabeth Vroman, whose novel *See How They Run* had been adapted into a Hollywood film. Even though she was publicized, Gwendolyn was unable to attend the event because she could not find a babysitter for baby Nora. Nora says now that her mother limited her travel until the child was eight or nine years old. Gwendolyn was a working mother who had it all, but negotiated how and when.

This is not to say she did not struggle between motherhood and writing. In December, 1951, when Hank was eleven and Nora a three-month-old infant, Gwendolyn confided in a letter to Langston Hughes that her duties and responsibilities as a mother were so overwhelming that she felt she was without time "to call my soul my own."[5] She barely had a moment for herself, much less to write. That is the story of most mothers who must care for their babies at home alone. And such is the predicament in which the artist who is a mother often finds herself. But Gwendolyn persisted through the most difficult years when her children were most dependent on her. And she provides a model for women who would take on these demanding dual roles of poet/writer and mother.

Amid the work of a literary life and the struggles and joys of wife-dom motherhood, Gwendolyn grappled with her family's housing situation. When she had received her prestigious award, they were living at 9134 South Wentworth Avenue, but the space was insufficient. Her husband Henry's partner at the auto shop had separated from his wife. So the Blakelys moved in with Henry's partner, with the wife's approval. That proved a gloomy business. Gwendolyn met with hostility from women neighbors who did not understand her working at home; nor did they understand the intellectual and creative nature of her work. She was not a schoolteacher or nurse, factory worker or day worker or clerical worker. She did not fit into their imaginations, if they had any. So they scorned her. One announced loud enough for Gwendolyn to overhear, "Like I say, if you worked for it, you could have it."[6]

That situation proved too much for Gwendolyn, so she and Hank (Gwendolyn and Henry had separated) moved into a rental property that the Blakelys owned in Kalamazoo, Michigan. But Gwendolyn hated the environment of people who appeared to her to be unimaginative, materialistic, "thing-minded." She missed the big city and its vibrancy and vitality, with so much to do and so many people to experience. So back to the city the family went.

In 1950, Gwendolyn was of the expressed opinion that a Negro poet's purpose as a person and writer was to be devoted to his or her craft. In an essay entitled "Poets Who Are Negroes," in a special issue of Atlanta University's journal *Phylon*, she famously stated:

> Every Negro poet has "something to say." Simply because he is a Negro; he cannot escape having important things to say. His mere body, for that matter, is an eloquence. His quiet walk down the street is a speech to the people. Is a rebuke, is a plea, is a school.
>
> But no real artist is going to be content offering raw materials. The Negro poet's most urgent duty, at present, is to polish his technique, his way of presenting his truths and beauties that these may be more insinuating, and, therefore, overwhelming.[7]

This statement would be used to definitively paint Gwendolyn as an artist absorbed in craft, eschewing action in the world. This is not entirely true. What is true is she believed poets and writers should be productive and devoted to their creative work so that their work might move people in the most profound and soul-stirring way.

In addition to her creative work, Gwendolyn pursued commercial work in the form of book reviews, work that had opened up since winning the Pulitzer. The *New York Herald Tribune* gave her a full page for her reviews.

Gwendolyn also wrote articles, including one for *Negro Digest* that addressed black women and marriage. In "Why Negro Women Leave Home," Gwendolyn wrote in a powerful, assertive manner, "A wife whose husband respects her as a person, instead of 'humoring' her as though she were a chattel or a slightly idiotic child, is not likely to leave him, despite his poverty, possible infidelity, or stupidity in other areas of their relationship. Women who cannot obtain such regard will increasingly prefer to live alone."[8]

In truth, Gwendolyn was of a brand of black women who, even in the most discriminatory of times, would separate themselves from husbands who disrespected them physically, verbally, or in other ways. Considering the times and the lack of career and work opportunities available to black women, as well as the limitations in housing and other necessities, embarking on their own was a bold move. Gwendolyn was one of the brave ones. Years later, black feminists would write the collection *All the Women Are White, All the Blacks Are Men: But Some of Us Are Brave*. Gwendolyn was a precursor in sentiment and strength.

"How I Told My Child About Race," also in *Negro Digest*, was Gwendolyn's account of the difficult rite of passage when a black mother must explain the matter of race to her black child. Gwendolyn was pleased that Hank maintained his openness to all races. In his adulthood, she would not be so pleased by this same openness.

It was the novelist Nelson Algren who recommended Gwendolyn for her largest assignment, for *Holiday* magazine. Growing up from infancy on a short street in Bronzeville and having lived in a variety of apartments in the Black Metropolis with her husband, Gwendolyn had more than a cursory knowledge of the space that Negro people inhabited. "They Call It Bronzeville" was written for *Holiday* in a special issue devoted entirely to Chicago. Langston Hughes, writing in the *Chicago Defender*, described Gwendolyn's article as "one of the finest pieces of reportage I have seen in a long time." On the other hand, Gertrude Martin, also in the *Defender*, felt that Gwendolyn "neglects the best and the worst." It might be safe to say that Gwendolyn focused on the everyday folks of Bronzeville who made up the majority.

Gwendolyn and Henry, now reunited, were hungry for a house after the birth of their second child, Nora. Once they had this goal in mind, Gwendolyn began to raise money.

She had started work on "American Family Brown," a series of poems, in the 1940s. The poems were rejected by Harper & Brothers in 1947 as passé in their topics of the socioeconomic problems of black people and the thorny issue of the de facto American apartheid. Having been assured by Elizabeth Lawrence that her writing fiction was not only in Harper & Brothers' best interest but in Gwendolyn's as well, Gwendolyn resurrected "American Family Brown" and set to work on reconstructing it as a novel. She had a goal in mind: to make enough money to buy her and Henry's dream house.

By January 1952, Gwendolyn had reworked "American Family Brown." The new title was *Bronzevillians*. (One wonders what happened to the collection of short stories *Under a Bronzeville Sky*, which she said she was working on, in a newspaper article in the 1940s.) Elizabeth Lawrence was pleased with this new submission and the direction in which Gwendolyn was taking it. She encouraged Gwendolyn to focus more on the people and the intersections of their lives. Gwendolyn kept revising, deciding to structure the work more around one family member and make other characters tangential to her, seen through her eyes.

Initially, the young woman protagonist was named Evelina. (Before that, when the story was first conceived, it was about the older, prettier sister, Helen.) Once Gwendolyn selected the homier name Maud Martha, the character revealed herself to the writer and the story flowed more freely. Gwendolyn mailed the final manuscript, now called *Maud Martha*, to Elizabeth Lawrence on September 15, 1952.

Meanwhile, Gwendolyn and Henry were saving their money to purchase a house. They sold their rental property in Kalamazoo, and Gwendolyn received a $500 advance for her novel. She hoped to sell individual chapters of it to *Harper's* and *Omnibook*, which had published portions of Ann Petry's novel about a young black woman, *The Street*. Other magazines she considered were *Reader's Digest* and *Life*, which had published portions of Ernest Hemingway's *The Old Man and the Sea*. Gwendolyn especially hoped to sell chapters to *Ebony*. So *Maud Martha* made the rounds at *Ebony*, *Life*, and *Mademoiselle*, where years before, Gwendolyn had been noted as a young woman of achievement. *Mademoiselle* took the longest to consider the manuscript, but no offers were made.

Still, the couple added to their savings with money from Gwendolyn's readings, reviews, and royalties, and, eventually, from a $500 loan from her parents, David and Keziah Brooks. Henry and Gwendolyn repaid the loan in small installments over the years. They had to take out a mortgage, but they moved into a house at 7428 South Evans on October 30, 1953, coincidentally, Hank's thirteenth birthday. Baby Nora was two years old.

Gwendolyn had been methodical in her pursuit of a home. She and Henry had chased their dream. Henry moved into a new business, a consumer consultant buying firm. Some things proceed slowly, but then there comes a surge. *Maud Martha* was about to make a decided wave with its publication.

Maud Martha is a nontraditional novel composed of thirty-four chapters focused on the title character. The novel covers Maud Martha Brown's girlhood, family, courtship, work experiences, experiences in the world, married life, neighbors, pregnancies, and motherhood.

The first twelve chapters are devoted to Maud Martha's girlhood. We first meet her as a little black girl who loves dandelions and enjoys a happy childhood with her mother; father; sister, Helen; and brother, Harry. She witnesses the death of her grandmother Ernestine. She anxiously awaits the visitation of a white boy from her school to her home, believing it to be a magnanimous "gift" to colored folks. She attends a stage show at the Regal Theater and the funeral of her uncle Tim. Maud Martha considers how different she is from her pretty sister, Helen. Maud Martha entertains a beau who is gifted with masculine charms that make him alluring to women. Then Maud Martha entertains a beau, black, a hanger-on who rather sadly wants to be a part of white intellectual society. Maud Martha's girlhood ends with the trip to New York where she moves outside her comfort zone and the confines of Bronzeville and explores a different world.

Or maybe the character's girlhood ends further on. Maud Martha talks seriously about marital selection with a third "low yellow" beau, Paul Phillips. She wants to "hook him." After marriage, as they plan their living quarters, Maud Martha and Paul argue over the kind of heating system that best suits their apartment. She deliberately chooses to follow the submissive female role by acceding to his wishes, believing that doing so is romantic. Later, she makes plans for the apartment's beautification, but those fall through. Perhaps her girlhood truly ended and womanhood began when she settles into the life she's been given.

The womanhood chapters of Maud Martha Brown Phillips are an examination of the imperfection of marriage, a realistic state. We see the young Phillipses at home; at the theater where they "are the only colored people" present and are painfully aware of being outsiders; at the Foxy Cats Ball, where Maud Martha confronts the colorist problem that clouds her marriage. (This chapter has often been reprinted.) Most hilarious and touching is the account of the birth of the couple's first child.

Maud Martha reflects on the bliss of her childhood and the dissatisfactions of her marriage. Her neighbors reflect the problems of poverty and race, from the latch-key child to the woman who claims to be a descendant of George Washington. Maud Martha runs into her second beau and glimpses another white intellectual world.

Chapter 25, "the self-solace" is also one of the most reprinted, expressing ways that black people deny overt racism to avoid dealing with it. A beauty-shop scene in which a white traveling saleswoman lets slip a racial slur is memorable and characteristic of the ways in which whites could conduct business in communities of color but not vice versa.

Mundane scenes add up to a well-lived life. But in addition to "the self-solace" and the visit to the all-white theater, three other scenes with whites explore Maud Martha's responses to racial insults: a millinery saleswoman who would rather not be waiting on a black woman is confronted by Maud Martha, who refuses to buy anything; Mrs. Burns-Cooper, who is chummy on one hand and too finicky on the other causes Maud Martha to flee; and, worst, the white Santa Claus who is interested in and charmed by white children and bored with and blind to the requests of Maud Martha's little girl. Santa Claus fills the black mother with rage.

Throughout it all, Maud Martha maintains her equanimity and sense of humor, even when her mother slights her for her prettier sister, Helen. Her brother, Harry, comes home from the war, and Maud Martha is pregnant. Life feels good to her and the reader as well.

Maud Martha is special because she is so poised, kind, intelligent, and genteel. Through her, the reader experiences issues of colorism, racism, and sexism in an intimate way that is not overwhelming. We are poised because Maud Martha is poised. And Maud Martha is poised because her creator, Gwendolyn Brooks, was.

Of *Maud Martha*, Gwendolyn said, "I wanted to give a picture of a girl growing up—a black girl growing up in Chicago, and of course much of it is wrenched from my own life and twisted. . . . I had written a few tiny stories, and felt that they would mesh, and I centered them and the others around one character. If there is a form, I would say it was imposed, at least in the beginning, when I started with these segments, or vignettes."[9]

Gwendolyn freely admitted that though *Maud Martha* was not an autobiographical novel, certain elements were taken from her life. For example, the character Emmanuel, who called Maud Martha "ole black gal" so scornfully, is taken from a real-life Emmanuel, who said the same words to the real-life Gwendolyn. The title "the self-solace" is taken from an actual incident in a beauty shop, which Gwendolyn found to be "mines of Life, organic, rich."[10]

Of the chapter "tree leaves leaving trees," Gwendolyn said it was based on her own experience, except that the child disregarded by the white Santa Claus was her son, not her daughter. However, the character of Maud Martha's husband, Paul Phillips, was not like that of Gwendolyn's husband, Henry, who was by no means rough-around-the-edges like Paul. That said, the chapter "a birth" was based on Henry's highly emotional reaction to the birth of their son.

When *Maud Martha* was in prepublication, it received early affirmative responses from the poets Robert Hillyer and Worth Tuttle Hedden. Ann Petry, author of *The Street*, also wrote a resoundingly positive response to the debut novel:

> I read *Maud Martha* with absolute delight in the beautiful structure of the book, delight in the way Maud Martha comes alive as a person caught up in timeless elemental situations.
>
> It was sheer reading pleasure to follow her development from childhood to adolescence, from courtship and marriage to the birth of her child—all of her experiences seemingly directed toward those final pages when she emerges as a full grown adult viewing the world with a philosophy of her own—compassionate, tender, brooding. All of it wonderful, all of it perfect![11]

Gwendolyn was most pleased by the response of another black woman novelist.

There was one negative response to *Maud Martha*, an underhanded one at that, from Inez Stark Boulton, who it would seem envisioned herself as a gatekeeper of race relations. She wrote Gwendolyn's editor, Elizabeth Lawrence, that she liked a great deal of *Maud Martha*, but

> from the point of view of most white readers it will be just another story of a Negro overcoming the tendency to have the chip knocked off her shoulder. . . . We are at the turning point, don't you think, where racial segregation should not be stressed, since so many advantages have been accorded Negroes in the last two years. My Negro friends in Washington, particularly the learned ones, are all vocal on this subject and agree that now is the time for negating any stories, poems or other propaganda showing ill treatment of Negroes.[12]

However, Langston Hughes wrote most succinctly and positively about the novel, praising it for being a work about a normal, young woman living a normal life, falling in love and marrying, and being somewhat happy, whereas he bemoaned the majority of novels by Negro people, saying they portrayed the most miserable aspects of existence. Gwendolyn's elegant normalcy remains the legacy of this nontraditional novel and its creator. Significantly, as the fiction of black women writers came to the fore, so too did *Maud Martha* experience a resurgence in popularity and find a new generation of readers, as well as a new publisher.

Gwendolyn's editor, Elizabeth Lawrence, believed *Maud Martha* missed "greatness" because its white characters were stock characters and not fully rounded. Until Gwendolyn was able to step beyond race as an artist and create convincing white characters, Lawrence stated, her work would suffer. George E. Kent, a biographer of Gwendolyn and a critic of William Faulkner, argued that Faulkner had not managed to create full black characters. He contended that authors are tied to their own experiences, and one's perceptions and historical roles make it difficult to create outside those roles.

Lawrence's beliefs aside, Gwendolyn creates for black characters the experience of racial insults and slights as perceived and experienced every day.

In 1954, Topeka, Kansas, Gwendolyn's birth place, became the subject of a Supreme Court decision overturning school segregation, *Brown v. the Board of Education*. As evidence of the necessity for integration, a "doll preference test," part of the testimony of Drs. Kenneth and Mamie Clark, was presented to the court. The doctors showed that a sizable number of Negro children, when asked to choose a doll that was beautiful and good and one that was not, invariably chose a white plastic doll rather than a brown plastic doll.

The doll test was a motivating factor for the Supreme Court to understand the deleterious effect of segregation and to order public schools nationwide desegregated "with all deliberate speed." The doll test also provided ample scientific evidence for Gwendolyn's experience and perception of a privilege based on color, even within Negro society. A sad but significant finding was that even in a 2010 study, white children overwhelmingly bestowed positive values on white dolls and black children still did too, though to a lesser extent.

But the mid-1950s would bring an event that would shake black America to its marrow and cause the sleeping dark giant to begin to stir.

Emmett Till was a fourteen-year-old black boy from Chicago who went to the Mississippi Delta in the summer of 1955 to visit relatives. One afternoon he walked into town to the corner store of Money, Mississippi, with his cousin. He was accused of whistling at a white woman and saying flirtatious words to her, a capital offense against the racist customs of the time. Decades later, the woman recanted her accusation. But that night, a group of white men, including the woman's husband, Roy Bryant, and his half-brother, J. W. Milan, invaded the home of Till's elderly great uncle and took the boy out. They had come in the dark with flashlights and guns. When Emmett Till was next seen, his bloated body had been dragged out of the Tallahatchie River. He had been beaten beyond recognition; his body mutilated. One of his eyes

oldiers were taken out of the ranks of the protective troops.
rborne was replaced with the Arkansas National Guard, feder-
by the president, and Central High School was integrated. But
tle Rock Nine continued to be abused and terrorized through-
eir school days. And the desegregation effort continued to be
ted throughout the city.

lolyn, always attentive to the times, followed these events from
go. She absorbed the tumult of change into her psyche and was
to take pen in hand.
ter Money, Mississippi, and Little Rock, Arkansas, who would
e affected? Even so, while the artist Gwendolyn was absorbing
ws from the South like an oyster absorbs sand and swirls it into
the quotidian Gwendolyn had to help her husband, Henry, meet
ortgage on their hard-earned house at 7428 South Evans.
ter the critical success of *Maud Martha*, Gwendolyn embarked on
creative projects to pursue because it was her nature to be cre-
y engaged and productive, and she needed the income. She at-
ted more fiction and suggested to her editor, Elizabeth Lawrence,
el with a male protagonist. "The Life of Lincoln West" went
gh several incarnations, though it wasn't published as a short story
1963 and later appeared as a poem in 1970. During this time,
ndolyn also wrote a collection of poems for children, *Bronzeville*
and Girls, published in 1956. These poems were warmly received
found to be universal, meaning whites could relate to them because
was nothing specifically black about them. In fact, the illustrations
onni Solbert were of white children. Gwendolyn was displeased
these joyous salutes to the happiness of so much of her childhood
given over to the realm of white children, while her own blackness
neglected and found unworthy to portray in illustrations.
Meanwhile, Henry and Gwendolyn worked as a unit to eliminate
cond mortgage. He had relegated his consulting work to morn-
and started as an assembly worker at Diamond T Trucks, where
would earn a promotion to foreman. They paid off the second

was missing; the other was hanging out of
had been cut off and his head chopped in f

His mother, Mamie Till Bradley, broug
cago, and he was prepared for public viewin
mother wanted the world to see what whit
done to her young son. The photo of the m
in *Jet* magazine and other black publications
ored people were shaken with sorrow and ra
were acquitted of the murder. Later, they b
that they had committed the murder, but the)
for the crime.

Four months later, in Montgomery, Al,
arrested for refusing to move to the back of
mett Till's murder and Rosa Park's arrest sp
America. The patterns of the past could not c
movement was on the rise.

After desegregation became the law of
pushed for integrated schools in cities through
Little Rock, Arkansas, the state capital, devel
plan for desegregation beginning with Centr
top black students, dubbed the Little Rock l
the school board to begin the process of integ
was met with strong resistance. The governor, (
the Arkansas National Guard to block the ni
Taunting, angry crowds gathered around the sch
students. One of the nine searched the mob for
into the eyes of an older white woman. The whit

The sight of the soldiers blocking black ch
school divided the nation. The school district c
and instituted a prayer vigil on September 12. P
senhower warned Governor Faubus to call off his
defiance of the Supreme Court's ruling. Little Ro
Mann, asked President Eisenhower to protect th
facilitate integration. Eisenhower sent the 101st

mortgage by January 1957. Also early that year, Harper's Juvenile Books solicited Gwendolyn to write a young adult novel about a teenage Negro girl growing up in Chicago. Gwendolyn did a great deal of work on the novel about a girl named Giovanna, growing up in the Mecca apartment building. Giovanna was a budding artist of some talent, but her family needed her to make a living to help support them. Giovanna tries to pursue her dream in spite of circumstances. Whether Gwendolyn wrote more of the story is not known, and the rest of the manuscript became lost. In any case, the young adult editor found the character and story appealing but the treatment too oblique.

The following year, Gwendolyn planned two books, a capsule course in poetry and a sequel to *Maud Martha*. Elizabeth Lawrence did not believe the capsule course, a short illustrated textbook, was broad enough in appeal. But *The Rise of Maud Martha* warranted more discussion, from Lawrence and from us now.

An excerpt from *The Rise of Maud Martha* was published in the original *Chicago* magazine. In the first chapter, Maud Martha is at the funeral of her husband, Paul, who has died in a fire. Ironically, and rather cruelly, his burnt blackness was likened to the blackness he so cruelly despised in others, perhaps even in Maud Martha. Maud Martha does not mourn his passing but is relieved and welcomes the freedom ahead of her. It is easy to see why Elizabeth Lawrence rejected this story. She suggested that Gwendolyn follow the same general plot but with a different protagonist. *The Rise of Maud Martha* is intrusive to the world of the original novel, said Lawrence; to see the characters come to such a catastrophic end, and for Paul to be judged with a harshness he did not seem to warrant, violates the mood of the first novel. Gwendolyn told Lawrence that she intended to "strain the story through the light of humor."[13] One can only wonder at the bitterness of the creator to choose so disastrous an end for Maud Martha's husband. Or did Gwendolyn see it as the hand of a just and vengeful God?

Gwendolyn continued to pursue other avenues for income and self-expression. She revealed more of her point of view on her personal idea of God in her article "What Prayer Did for Me," published in the *Chicago American*, February 26, 1958. With little Nora in mind, she had prayed for a dying child and the child had been healed. Gwendolyn affirmed that she had felt "a strength superior to any I had known." She was not routinely a church-goer, but she found the divine in everything and every living being: plants, sky, squirrels, mice, lizards, and the wind that cannot be seen. When discussing "brotherly love," a chapter from *Maud Martha*, she expanded on her ideas about creatures and living things with cosmic empathy: "my continuing feelings that chickens are people, as are dogs, cats, rats, ants, birds, snakes, roaches, bears, fish, trees, weeds, flowers. People, that is, in the sense that we conceive people to be: things of identity and response."[14] Although she failed in her attempt to revise the story of Giovanna—entitled *In the Mecca*—as an adult novel about a biracial young woman, what she did write reflects another dimension of her ideas of the workings of the universe.

The white mother feeling doomed by her marriage to a Negro man wants her daughter to marry a white man. Her father wants her to wed a steady, workaday man of color. Her Negro grandmother wants her to work hard. Giovanna weds for love and bears a child. Her white mother murders the child. The white mother and Negro grandmother are burned black in a fire. Later, Giovanna and her two children by her black husband visit the Mecca building, which is being torn down.

Again, Gwendolyn's just and vengeful God punishes those guilty of color prejudice and, in this case, murder. This version of *In the Mecca* was rejected by Harper for a number of reasons, most notably, its melodrama and forced conclusion.

Gwendolyn would meet greater success with her next book of poetry, portions of which she sent to her editor almost as soon as the rejected novel was returned. Elizabeth Lawrence did not like the title *Bronzeville Men and Women* for the new poems, but she found "superb stuff" and "major achievements" in what Gwendolyn had sent her, including poems about Emmett Till and Little Rock.[15]

The title of the book, her third collection of adult poetry, was now *The Bean Eaters*. Gwendolyn worked industriously on additional poems to flesh out the collection to meet a publication date in the following year. She also submitted poems for publication in *Harper's* and *Poetry* magazines. Significantly *Poetry* published what became the most well-known of the poems: "The Bean Eaters," "We Real Cool," "Old Mary," and "Strong Men Riding Horses." *Harper's* published "The Explorer" and "For Clarice It Is Terrible Because with This He Takes Away All the Popular Songs and the Moonlights and Still Night Hushes and the Movies with Star-Eyed Girls and Simpering Males." The titles alone indicate that Gwendolyn was off in a direction different from her first two volumes, something tougher, edgier.

> *They eat beans mostly, this old yellow pair.*
> *Dinner is a casual affair.*

The title poem, "The Bean Eaters," is a classic "newsreel" poem describing in the third person, omniscient, an elderly couple at the dinner table, eating beans in solitude and remembering with feelings of joy and regret past and better times.

The phrase "the bean eaters" is global. In her autobiography, Gwendolyn wrote that in times when her father's earnings were diminished by the Depression, the family's dinner menu was changed from meat, potatoes, and vegetables to simply beans. In pre-vegetarian times, beans were the symbol of poverty. Gwendolyn's characters consumed "navy beans and tomato catsup." This is significant because Gwendolyn is subtly addressing the idea of economic class, the people who are in a state of want, the people who go without.

WE REAL COOL
    The Pool Players.
    Seven at the Golden Shovel.

> *We real cool. We*
> *Left school. We*

Lurk late. We
Strike straight. We

Sing sin. We
Thin gin. We

Jazz June. We
Die soon.

"We Real Cool" is Gwendolyn's most well-known poem. It is a model of compression, economy, and rhythm. More importantly, it is an unforgettable portrait of lost young men of color whose lives are over far too soon. The poem is unusual because it is in a collective voice, that of a group of young black men estranged from their community. They have given up hope of advancement through education. Indeed, they have given up hope of a future. Gwendolyn said the "we" should be said softly, perhaps as a sign of diminishment. These young men are not thriving. Lurking, they hang in shadows, never in the sun of their manhood. Striking, they bring harm to each other and possibly others in the community. They sing sin, celebrating negativity in a hedonistic way. They drink and carouse. They jazz June, living unfettered in the spring of their lives, which are over too soon. Gwendolyn does not mince words. These young men die from homicide or neglect, medical or social. The impact of the poem lies in its indictment of a society that has alienated these young black men. It is a protest poem, as powerful as Wright's *Native Son* or an essay by James Baldwin. Gwendolyn's social consciousness was building. Once she said that poverty provoked her imagination. But it also provoked her outrage, more than she herself might even have known.

The seed for the satirical "Lovers of the Poor" was planted when Gwendolyn was awarded the Pulitzer Prize. Inquisitive suburban white women searched out her home and made their way there. Their attitude was so offensive to Gwendolyn that the poem grew out of that encounter with the high-toned, supercilious practitioners of "loathe-love," a false regard for black life as unworthy and indecent in the extreme, surpassing the haughtiness of the wealthy ladies.

The poem describes the visit of the "Ladies from the Ladies' Betterment League" to a large, run-down tenement, a visit designed for charity. The ladies were "full, / Sleek, tender-clad, fit, fiftyish, a-glow, all / Sweetly abortive, hinting at fat fruit." These ladies are rich, well cared for, and not life-giving. After all, they are a dreadful mix of sugar and the stoppage of life. They want to give to the "worthy poor." The worthy poor must not be "too swarthy," too dark or dirty, or bold enough to look them straight in the eye. The Ladies are repelled:

> *But it's all so bad! and entirely too much for them.*
> *The stench; the urine, cabbage, and dead beans,*
> *Dead porridges of assorted dusty grains,*
> *The old smoke, heavy diapers, and, they're told,*
> *Something called chitterlings. The darkness. Drawn*
> *Darkness, or dirty light. The soil that stirs.*

The Ladies are not prepared for "children children children." They race away, not deigning to graze the walls of the hall. They decide to mail some money to these poor people. These unworthy poor.

The poem must be read aloud to obtain the full benefit of its comedic undertone. It makes mincemeat of certain well-meaning suburbanites, but the reader savors it with delight. Gwendolyn attacks the issues of race and class with a vengeance. In the realm of the spirit, she comments on the superficiality of charity that does not come from the heart. She denounces materialism and the absence of compassion and basic understanding of the broad spectrum of humanity. People who are different from us are no less worthy; people who have less are not less; and people who do not act as we do are not less than we are. Kindness is the most important thing. In fact, Gwendolyn Brooks believed in a "church of kindness."

She was a mother who loved not only her children but all children. When she spoke of a Bronzeville mother, she could have been referring to herself. "A Bronzeville Mother Loiters in Mississippi, Meanwhile, A Mississippi Mother Burns Bacon" focuses on Carolyn Bryant, the white woman whom Emmett Till allegedly whistled at, who was the prime cause of the murder but not the murderer. This poem is her intense reflection on how far removed from her chivalrous redemption was the murder of a child.

Immediately following this poem from the white mother's guilty perspective is "The Last Quatrain of the Ballad of Emmett Till," a companion piece focusing on Emmett's bereaved mother.

> *(after the murder,*
> *after the burial)*
> *Emmett's mother is a pretty-faced thing*
> *the tint of pulled taffy.*
> *She sits in a red room,*
> *drinking black coffee.*
> *She kisses her killed boy.*
> *And she is sorry.*
> *Chaos in windy grays*
> *through a red prairie. . . .*

Mamie Till Bradley is pretty, sweet, and tense with held-in emotion. The red room she sits in may be a bleeding womb or a room symbolic of bloody deeds. Phonetically, "red room" is close to "murder" spelled backwards.

Black coffee is bitter. The mother of the murdered black boy drinks a bitter brew; she is bitter. Because the poem takes place after the murder and after the burial, when she kisses her killed boy, it is in memory or a photograph. She is sorry that she may have indirectly brought his end. By sending him south, to be away from the streets of Chicago, she sent him to the place where he was brutally slain and tied with barbed wire. This divergence between her intention and the result is chaos. Grief sweeps through the North and the red prairie with the news of murder. Black people mourned en masse.

In these few lines, Gwendolyn captured the mood of Afro-America. Grief gave way to outrage. And as the people of the Black Lives Matter movement say after a contemporary lynching, "Enough is enough," black people then were moved to set change in motion.

"Between 1945 and 1954, at least nine major race riots occurred in Chicago."[16] Invariably, the riots were precipitated by the problem of territory. Whites did not want black people to live in or even walk through white areas. Major incidents were sparked when Negro families moved to white neighborhoods. Such an incident is anticipated in Lorraine Hansberry's *A Raisin in the Sun*, when the Younger family bravely sets out to move into all-white and unwelcoming Clybourne Park. Gwendolyn captures such an incident in progress in "The Ballad of Rudolph Reed."

> *Rudolph Reed was oaken.*
> *His wife was oaken too.*
> *And his two good girls and his good little man*
> *Oakened as they grew.*
>
> *"I am not hungry for berries.*
> *I am not hungry for bread.*
> *But hungry hungry for a house*
> *Where at night a man in bed*
>
> *"May never hear the plaster*
> *Stir as if in pain.*
> *May never hear the roaches*
> *Falling like fat rain. . . .*

Rudolph Reed finds a house at a decent price and buys it from an unscrupulous realtor who knows the trouble Reed and his family will face in their new neighborhood. And the Reeds do meet trouble. Their neighbors harass and menace them over three nights. On the third night, a neighbor sends a rock through a window. It strikes one of Reed's daughters. Reed has had enough. He runs out into the night, armed and ready to fight, to defend his family.

> *By the time he had hurt his fourth white man*
> *Rudolph Reed was dead.*
> *His neighbors gathered and kicked his corpse.*
> *"Nigger—" his neighbors said.*

When Martin Luther King Jr. marched with protesters for fair housing through all-white Marquette Park in 1966, he was hit with a rock that caused him to stumble. This was in broad daylight. Gwendolyn's imaginary Rudolph Reed could easily have been slain in this way in Chicago a few years earlier.

Understanding Gwendolyn's heritage and placing her work in comparable bop terms of Miles Davis and Thelonious Monk, novelist and friend Frank London Brown wrote in the *Chicago Defender* June 21, 1960, "Gwendolyn Brooks is from the set. . . . She grew up on the stroll. She has seen and known the cool ones, and the down ones, and the ones with dark glasses 'round 'bout midnight." Gwendolyn's daughter, Nora, attests to the fact that her mother would put on some music and go "diddy bopping" around the house. The music had to have been jazz as its rhythms and meter permeated Gwendolyn's earliest works.

Brown knew Gwendolyn's history and he understood her needs as a creative writer. He made a case for her to a black audience in the *Chicago Defender*, July 21, 1960, saying that the community was neglecting its writers and musicians. He named Gwendolyn as a prime example of a valuable asset who might have to find more resources elsewhere. He was determined to create resources for her.

Brown tried unsuccessfully to obtain for Gwendolyn a teaching position at Roosevelt University in downtown Chicago. She completed application forms, but it would seem she was turned down for the job because she did not have a college degree. She only had a

Pulitzer Prize, a strong publishing history, and experience as a judge of national and local literary contests. Brown did not give up on his mission to help Gwendolyn secure employment in teaching, which she did want. Six days before his untimely death from leukemia, on March 6, 1962, Gwendolyn was hired to teach American literature in the University of Chicago's Union Leadership Program, where Brown was a director. She would teach seven sessions that spring, from April to May.

Gradually, Gwendolyn waded into the pool of teaching. In 1963, she would dive in at the behest of one Mirron (Mike) Alexandroff, president of Columbia College Chicago, a downtown institution specializing in writing, film, theater, dance, and visual arts. Alexandroff hired her to teach a poetry workshop, saying, "Do anything you want with it. Take it outdoors. Take it to a restaurant—run it in a restaurant, a coffee shop. Do absolutely anything you want with it. *Any-thing.*"[17] Alexandroff was a supporter of excellence, experimentation, and the arts, and Gwendolyn Brooks was an artist of the first order, degree or no degree. Her credentials were in her craft. This was the way Columbia College recognized its faculty then.

Gwendolyn understood why a teaching assignment had been so long in coming to her, saying, "Because no one ever asked me before. . . . I guess because I have three strikes on me. I am a woman. I am a Negro. And I have no college degree." The writer of the newspaper column wherein this comment may be found wrote in response, "None of these reasons is big enough, except in the minds of small men."[18]

Gwendolyn had assessed the situation accurately, but even she did not fully appreciate how deep and systematic were the weights against blacks, women, and artists in the academy. Zora Neale Hurston had a degree and a publishing history, and she found it difficult to be employed as a teacher. In her later years, she worked as a hotel maid. Margaret Walker Alexander had presciently pursued a PhD and a steady, full-time teaching position but had also given up time to write.

Alexandroff had opened a door for Gwendolyn, and the poet walked through as a teacher in a new blue suit. "Twenty-one young souls were sitting there, awaiting the knowledge, the magic, the definitions that I was bringing them surely. I felt the need to spin automatically around and leave within the minute of my arrival. But I stayed, and discovered that it was possible to enjoy this thing that I had never done before."[19] But the role of teacher came instinctively to her. Understanding the concept that *poeta nascitur, non fit* (a poet is born, not made), she took on her mission to allow poets to reveal themselves and lovers of poetry to gain skill in writing and understanding.

She taught at Columbia College once a week in the fall, spring, and some summers until the winter of 1969. Afterward, she taught at Elmhurst College (Elmhurst, Illinois); Northeastern Illinois State College, on the north side of Chicago; and the University of Wisconsin at Madison as a professor of English. She taught freshman English, Twentieth-Century Poetry and the Short Story, and poetry, fiction, and creative-writing workshops. Columbia College had given her entrance to a new field. She was a good teacher who took her job seriously.

Gwendolyn asked of her students no more than she asked of herself: mastery of forms, technical proficiency, and then the extension of technique. They were required to write twenty poems during the semester, half of these formal. They learned Petrarchan, Shakespearean, and Spenserian sonnet forms; Japanese Haiku and tanka; ballads, free and blank verse, and verse play. And they learned to defy form by studying the poetry of the Beat writers.

Poetry classes were enlivened with discussion, debate, poetry on record, music on record, writing in response to music, and peer criticism. Gwendolyn's fiction-writing classes were just as rigorous, requiring that students complete short stories, a novella, or the beginning of a novel. She even demanded at Elmhurst that her students read a lengthy work of literary criticism.

With her attention to craft and the development of students' creative sensibility, perhaps she was trying to cultivate what Martin Luther King Jr. would say African Americans needed to survive: "a tough mind and a tender heart." They would need these.

The late 1950s and early 1960s brought events that would register on Gwendolyn's personal Richter scale: her father, David, passed away November 21, 1959; *The Bean Eaters*, published in 1960, would be the last book of entirely new poems that Gwendolyn would publish at Harper & Brothers; her *Selected Poems* was brought out with some new poems in 1963; and Elizabeth Lawrence, her long-time editor at Harper, retired. Her new editors were Genevieve Young and Ann Harris, with whom Gwendolyn was acquainted.

Gwendolyn dedicated *The Bean Eaters* to her father and entered the decade on a somber note. She and Lawrence had enjoyed a fruitful relationship as writer and editor for twenty years. They worked together well, even though Lawrence had continued to urge Gwendolyn to pursue "universality."

Few poems reflect the changes of the years from 1960 to 1963. These are incorporated in *Selected Poems* in the section "1963." The most richly developed is dedicated to the Freedom Riders, "Riders to the Blood-Red Wrath." The poem is a journey through the hostile territory of American apartheid, back in time through the slave trade. Brooks offers awareness that cruelties have been done against more people than Negro people. The Freedom Rider will ride until man's inhumanity against man is ended. The poem has pulse and passion; its language is dense and layered with meaning. It requires rereading.

> *My proper prudence toward his proper probe*
> *Astonished their ancestral seemliness.*
> *It was a not-nice risk, a wrought risk, was*
> *An indelicate risk, they thought. And an excess.*

So the Freedom Rider sets out as the racist segregationists look on.

Gwendolyn also liked to explore love themes. In "To Be in Love," we travel though the magic of the love experience, lifting and falling in disappointment at the discovery of the lover's flaws. The poem itself is a love experience.

A poem that may be close to Gwendolyn and Henry's at-home life is "Big Bessie throws her son into the street." It reflects their experience with their son Hank, who left home when he would not abide by the rules of the house.

> *A day of sunny face and temper.*
> *The winter trees*
> *Are musical.*
>
> *Bright lameness from my beautiful disease,*
> *You have your destiny to chip and eat.*
>
> *Be precise.*
> *With something better than candles in the eyes.*
> *(Candles are not enough.)*
>
> *At the root of the will, a wild inflammable stuff.*
>
> *New pioneer of days and ways, be gone.*
> *Hunt out your own or make your way alone.*
>
> *Go down the street.*

The day is portentous, not necessarily bad, and Big Bessie, a recurring character, has had enough of her son. She wants him out on his own with more than just high hopes. She wants him to prove his mettle. It is time for him to be a man and on his own two feet. The Blakelys were probably not so firm as Big Bessie, but more than likely they were relieved when Hank left home and went first to the YMCA, then to an apartment on the North Side, then to the Marines.

One critical response to *Selected Poems* was especially noteworthy because it lit a fire that raged for decades. In the October 27, 1963, Book

Week section of the *New York Herald Tribune*, Louis Simpson opined, "Gwendolyn Brooks' *Selected Poems* contains some lively pictures of Negro life. . . . I am not sure it is possible for a Negro to write well without making us aware he is a Negro; on the other hand, if being a Negro is the only subject, the writing is not important." It is safe to say that Simpson's opinion was dismissed on any number of counts.

Throughout the 1950s and early 1960s, Gwendolyn and Henry had moved in an integrated circle of friends who were writers and artists. She maintained an awareness of change, and she believed wholeheartedly that full integration would be the solution to problems for Negro people and America.

She was excited when the youth of her block club, a neighborhood association, confronted a local Hi-Lo grocery store over discrimination in hiring. When the grocery store turned a deaf ear to the letter the block club had sent, Gwendolyn's young neighbor organized a picket line. The hiring practices were changed. She admired young people. Perhaps they reminded her of her own days as a young activist.

In the years ahead, young black people would lead her through a personal earthquake and onto the other side of new, higher ground.

CHAPTER SIX

Black Is Beautiful

A tremor shook Gwendolyn as she made her way to higher ground: she was misquoted by a newspaperman from the *San Jose Mercury News* who said that she "admits she had to turn down requests from civil rights groups to save her literary integrity. 'They wanted me to write marching songs,' Miss Brooks said. 'I just couldn't do that.'"[1] Gwendolyn had said no such thing. In fact, she considered what the reporter claimed she had said as traitorous to her race.

In *Negro Digest*, Gwendolyn denounced the misrepresentation of herself as an artist divorced from the pulse of the people, too elevated to write "marching songs." To her mind, she would have been proud to have penned "We Shall Overcome." She did not relish being counted out of the struggle. She wanted to be at the heart of it. Something in her was open for the disruption of a move to higher ground and the people who dwelled there. She liked to be where the action was. She told her biographer, George E. Kent, that she "liked people who did things."[2] It would seem she was ready to do things, whether she said so or not.

She had thought it would be a writers' conference like any other, in spite of the contentious flare-ups over race at conferences in recent years. She had thought she would do her part and that the audience would be appropriately responsive to her reading.

Gwendolyn arrived at the Second Annual Fisk Writers Conference, organized by the novelist John Oliver Killens, in the spring of 1967 in Nashville, Tennessee, thinking she would be as warmly received as she had been at her previous reading in cold, all-white South Dakota. At Fisk she was to read with her old friend from the Visionaries workshop, Margaret Danner. Poet Amiri Baraka—formerly known as LeRoi Jones—was there as a playwright, speaking with Detroit's Ron Milner; Chicago novelist Ronald Fair presented with John Oliver Killens; and Chicago historian Lerone Bennett Jr. spoke with New York's John Henrik Clarke. These participants addressed the conference theme, "The Black Writer and Human Rights."

John Henrik Clarke noted the change in names, that Negroes were calling themselves Afro-Americans. They had been "black" people for some time now. But Gwendolyn Brooks was still calling herself and her people "Negroes." Lerone Bennett spoke of the black writer's role as a revolutionary, of the necessity to redefine himself outside the realm of white supremacist values and to cast the civil rights struggle in the realm of revolution, beginning with black writers addressing black people instead of their oppressors. These were radical messages.

Gwendolyn felt the electricity in the air. The young people who attended the workshops were different. They were self-confident, awe-inspiring. They would impress Gwendolyn Brooks as black and beautiful. They were on fire with the fever of a proud sense of heritage and mission. They were the children of Malcolm X—independent of the need for white approval or acceptance, bold and clamoring to knock down American customs that denied them fullness as human beings.

Yet when Gwendolyn and Margaret Danner were set to read, Danner began with a preamble, chastising the young man who had introduced them. He had zealously called for a poetry like that of the Harlem Renaissance, politically engaged and in touch with the black man's struggle. Danner informed him that he had not read the black poetry that was available to him. She instructed him to read their work. Then she read.

Gwendolyn followed with her own brief reprimand and begged off from "wring[ing] the neck of the introducer."[3] She gave a brief speech on heritage and the need for human variety. She left them with these words: "Poetry . . . must be the result of involvement with emotions and idea and ink and paper." Then she read her poems "Malcolm X," "Boy Breaking Glass," "kitchenette building," "the mother," "Negro Hero," the second sonnet from "children of the poor," "Beverly Hills, Chicago," and "We Real Cool," which was deeply appreciated. She rounded off her program with "The Ballad of Rudolph Reed" and the last stanza of "Riders to the Blood-Red Wrath." Finally, she read the prose version of "The Life of Lincoln West." She admitted that she was "a Lincoln West" and laughed at this "Ugliest little boy that everyone ever saw." She laughed just as the audience had laughed.[4]

The Gwendolyn portion of the program ended with Oscar Brown Jr. singing his arrangement of her poem "of DeWitt Williams on his way to Lincoln Cemetery." As the song was ending, Amiri Baraka walked in and Gwendolyn called attention to his entrance. The audience hailed him as a brilliant and beloved crown prince.

After Gwendolyn and Cunningham gave their readings to obliging and sometimes appreciative applause, they wandered through the conference in a state of wonder and befuddlement. Gwendolyn said, "In my cartoon-basket I keep a cartoon of a dowager-furred Helen Hokinson woman. She is on parade in the world. She is a sign-carrier in the wild world. Her sign says, 'Will someone please tell me what is going on?.' . . . In 1967's Nashville, however, the somewhat dotty expression in the eyes of the cartoon-woman, the *agapeness*, [was] certainly mine. I was in some inscrutable and uncomfortable wonderland."[5] She had never before encountered such young black people, who were so casually confident, so fiery, focused, and determined to remake the world.

Baraka, their hero, shouted, "Up against the wall, white man!" Gwendolyn describes drums and "underhumming" at his and Ron

Milner's theater presentation. "Up against the wall. And a pensive (until that moment) white man of thirty or thirty three abruptly shot himself into the heavy air, screaming 'Yeah! Yeah! Up against the wall, Brother! KILL 'EM ALL! KILL 'EM ALL!'"[6]

Gwendolyn watched with interest as the young white man yelled excitedly for his own extermination.

She was as moved in her own way by Baraka and these children of Malcolm X with their fierce pride, great sense of purpose, and powerful sense of dignity and self-definition. She felt that she had walked to a high ground, and she wanted to see more of what was going on.

When Gwendolyn, in a state of high excitement, returned home after her revelation at Fisk, she found waiting for her a telegram inviting her to the preview of a play by Oscar Brown Jr. This play was *Opportunity Please Knock*. Brown was a singer, playwright, poet, composer, activist, and actor. He was noted for songs like "Brown Baby," sung by Mahalia Jackson, and "Work Song" and "Bid 'Em In," sung by Nina Simone. He collaborated with Max Roach on the album *We Insist!* as an affirmation of the freedom struggle of black America. Of course, he had set at least one of Gwendolyn's poems to music.

Gwendolyn had been acquainted with Brown as early as 1949, when he was one of the actors in the radio play about her. Brown was anxious for her to see *Opportunity Please Knock*, so Gwendolyn went to the preview with her teenaged daughter, Nora, and one of Nora's friends.

The musical generated more excitement in Gwendolyn, still energized by her adventure at Fisk. In addition, for some time she had wanted to do something for the youth who appeared in Brown's play. They were Blackstone Rangers, members of an increasingly notorious teenage street gang. Perhaps they caused Gwendolyn to think of her own words, "We real cool. We die soon." And she wanted to do something to forestall empty fate, not simply to write about it but to, in some way, stop it.

After viewing *Opportunity Please Knock*, she praised the show to Brown and asked, "Are there any writers among them? Because I'd like to have a workshop for them, if any of them are interested."

As it turned out, certain of the gang members had expressed an interest in writing and wanted to know if Gwendolyn would like to read their manuscripts. Brown contacted Walter Bradford, a student at Woodrow Wilson Junior College, where Gwendolyn had studied. Walter was in his twenties and worked with teens. He assembled seven or eight young people for a workshop that met in First Presbyterian Church in Woodlawn. They—members of the Blackstone Rangers gang and Gwendolyn—met every Friday downstairs. The cast of *Opportunity Please Knock* was upstairs rehearsing.

In that first meeting and in others thereafter, workshop members read their poems. "They used to laugh at me to beat the band for being interested in the sonnet and trying to teach them iambic pentameter," Gwendolyn said.[7]

One participant in that first meeting, Don L. Lee (later known as Haki Madhubuti), had already self-published a book, *Think Black*. Lee was a young Army veteran, self-educated from extensive reading, and now in college. He was mentored by Gwendolyn's old friend Margaret Burroughs and her husband, Charles. Lee liked what he saw at that first workshop with the Blackstone Rangers, so he came back for the second. He met Walter Bradford at the second session, and the two of them would prove to have a long-standing, family-like relationship with Gwendolyn.

Gwendolyn recalled of the workshop that after "about six or eight months after we started, I quit and we just became friends." Having given all that she could to the expressive Blackstone Rangers, Gwendolyn turned the writing group over to Walter Bradford. She provided Bradford with guides and literature to help him sustain the group, and she supported their literary needs financially. Bradford, in turn, developed a workshop of twenty members that thrived.

Whereas Bradford continued with the most serious high school-age writers, Gwendolyn opened her home once a month to a group of college students with literary aspirations, including the aforementioned Lee. This group of older writers came from teen organizers and Woodrow Wilson Junior College students to whom Walter introduced her.

These were Alicia Johnson, Jim Taylor, Mike Cook, Peggy Susberry, Sharon Scott (the one high schooler), Kharlos Tucker (later Sigemonde Wimberli), Ronda Davis, Jewel Latimore (later Johari Amini), Jim Cunningham, Carolyn Rodgers, Doris Turner, and Carol Clark.

Nothing was the same for Gwendolyn once she had opened her door for these purveyors of the new blackness. What had struck her at Fisk was now sitting in her living room commanding her attention. It was a mutual love affair.

Don Lee, now Haki Madhubuti, remembers, "It was an honor to be in her house. She lived like us. A small wood frame house, small kitchen, small living room packed with books."

She taught them craft; they had no interest in writing for white people, or in hearing what white people had to say about their work. They taught Gwendolyn the way the world now worked. She had some understanding, but it was limited in their eyes. They wanted her to see things from a black position, without equivocation. They wanted her to understand the systemic nature of racism, how it was rooted in white hegemony, a rock-hearted white supremacy, and that supremacy was undergirded by economic exploitation and inequity. Gwendolyn was standing on a mountaintop and could now see in all directions.

Slowly, they influenced her. Without their telling her to, she let her hair be in its natural state, an Afro, and so announced that she was standing up for being black.

Gwendolyn did not readily fall in step with the young blacks. There were rich arguments at the Blakely home between Gwendolyn and the trailblazers. They were powerfully anti-white people, whereas Gwendolyn believed in the intrinsic goodness of all humanity; hers was an integrationist point of view. When she protested the blanket denunciation of all white persons, they disputed her. Gwendolyn and Henry still had trusted white friends like Bob and Alice Cromie, he a journalist and broadcaster, with whom they had traveled, lecturing and vacationing; and Beryl and Gene Zitch of Contemporary Forum, which served as Gwendolyn's booking agency.

The workshop participants condemned the history of white extermination of indigenous peoples, enslavement, the exploitation and degradation of black people, brutality and murderous acts in the civil rights struggle, and mass destructiveness. The young poets moved into a strict Black Nationalist position, focusing on a love of black folks, a call for the development of black people, believing in the inevitable need for independence and autonomy from white people. That undertaking not being immediate, they focused on literary concerns. The belief was and is that *nommo*—a Bantu word for the power of language to make change—preceded and precipitated action.

They argued about the creation of a body of literature designed to wake up black people to blackness and the need for black unity and liberation. How best to do that in words was the question. Val Gray Ward, a talented actress and interpreter of Afro-American literature, and a friend of Gwendolyn's, objected to the unnecessary use of profanity in the new black poetry. She found the use of curse words, especially the most profane "motherfucker" off-putting to a good portion of the black audience. Lee objected to the objection.

The group debated this furiously, as they did many issues. They embarked on a quest to determine if their works were "black." Gwendolyn mediated these literary arguments. She was in the quest with them. Somewhere along the way, they had begun to refer to her as Gwen, indicating their affection for her and sense of familial regard.

The Committee for the Arts began meeting in Chicago in 1966. In 1967, it would become the Organization of Black American Culture (OBAC). Its members included Gerald McWorter (later known as Abdul Alkalimat), sociologist; Jeff Donaldson, visual artist; Conrad Kent Rivers, poet; Joseph Robinson, community organizer; E. Duke McNeil, attorney; and Hoyt W. Fuller, editor of *Negro Digest*, long known to Gwendolyn. Also known to Gwendolyn was Ann McNeil (later Dr. Ann Smith), whom Gwendolyn had met at Northeastern Illinois University, when both were teaching there.

The idea behind OBAC was the belief that art has properties that would heal and restore the collective psyche of the black citizens of Chicago, so as to enable them to achieve political and socioeconomic empowerment. In other words, OBAC's goal was to create art that makes people whole and self-determining. OBAC was named by Jeff Donaldson after the Yoruba word *Oba*, meaning chief or leader. OBAC was divided into several workshops on the visual arts, writing, community organizing, and drama, whose presentations were overseen by Ann McNeil. There was no music workshop as the Association for the Advancement of Creative Musicians already existed. OBAC's drama presentations did not compete with Val Gray Ward's Kuumba Theater.

OBAC's visual arts workshop was headed by Jeff Donaldson, later dean of the College of Fine Arts at Howard University. Participants in that workshop painted the famed Wall of Respect, an outdoor mural celebrating black heroes. This mural, painted on the side of a building at Forty-Third and Langley Avenue, would spark a mural movement across America. The Wall of Respect was dedicated on August 27, 1967, a singular public event for Gwendolyn, aligning her with a new breed of black people. Portrayed were Gwendolyn, Lerone Bennett Jr., H. Rap Brown, W. E. B. Du Bois, James Baldwin, Stokely Carmichael, Wilt Chamberlain, Ornette Coleman, John Coltrane, Amiri Baraka, John Oliver Killen, Martin Luther King Jr., Malcolm X, Thelonious Monk, Max Roach, Nina Simone, and Sarah Vaughan. The Wall of Respect also carried Baraka's poem "S.O.S.," which called to all blacks to help form a black solidarity.[8] The community had chosen its own heroes.

The most long-standing of the OBAC workshops was the writer's workshop, chaired by Hoyt W. Fuller. Among the founding members were Don Lee, Carolyn Rodgers, Jewel Latimore (later known as Johari Amini), Cecil Brown, and Ronald Fair. Gwendolyn's workshop and OBAC overlapped for a time. A literary movement was on.

Unfortunately, her longtime mentor and friend Langston Hughes would not be there for it. He passed away after surgery on May 22,

1967. He had been a source of support and inspiration from the generation before her.

Gwendolyn had been haunted by her experiences at the Mecca building for decades. She had attempted to capture the edifice and its inhabitants in fiction several times but had not been successful. On August 29, 1962, Elizabeth Lawrence had written to Gwendolyn, "Good! I am not surprised that you must get The Mecca out of your system, and I believe that poetry will serve you better than prose."[9]

It would not be until September 1967 that Gwendolyn's poetic version of *In the Mecca* would be delivered to what was now Harper & Row (previously Harper & Brothers). When it arrived, it was not well received by its first reader. By that time, Lawrence had retired and would have to be called in to review this new, artistically controversial work. Harper asked for additional poems for the "After Mecca" section. Gwendolyn obliged. Harper & Row published *In the Mecca* in 1968, a most momentous American year.

As a kind of preface to the poem "In the Mecca," Gwendolyn opened with a quote from the author John Bartlow Martin describing the Mecca building:

> a great gray hulk of brick, four stories high, topped by an ungainly smokestack, ancient and enormous, filling half the block north of Thirty-fourth Street between State and Dearborn . . . The Mecca Building is U-shaped. The dirt courtyard is littered with newspapers and tin cans, milk cartons and broken glass. . . . Iron fire escapes run up the building's face and ladders reach from them to the roof. There are four main entrances, two on Dearborn and two on State Street. At each is a gray stone threshold and over each is carved "THE MECCA."

In the Mecca was dedicated "To the memory of Langston Hughes; and to James Baldwin, Amiri Baraka, and Mike Alexandroff, educators

extraordinaire." It also was dedicated "IN TRIBUTE—Jim Cunning-
ham, Jim Taylor, Mike Cook, Walter Bradford, Don Lee, Curtis Ellis,
Roy Lewis, Peggy Susberry, Ronda Davis, Carolyn Rodgers, Sharon
Scott, Alicia Johnson, Jewel Latimore." Gwendolyn had acknowledged
two generations of visionaries and cultural workers who had impacted
the evolution of her own black and increasingly urgent consciousness.
The long work on the volume had progressed as the poet herself had
progressed on her path to greater political awareness.

In the Mecca is an extended narrative that is a mystery. The frame
story is the search for a missing child. Along the way to her discovery,
the reader encounters a rich variety of characters who dwell in the
huge edifice of 176 apartments. Gwendolyn introduces us to the in-
habitants of many of those apartments, including Mrs. Sallie Smith,
the mother of the lost Pepita.

The opening lines of "In the Mecca" are portentous and commanding.

Sit where the light corrupts your face,
Mies Van der Rohe retires from grace.
And the fair fables fall.

It is conceivable that the poet is transforming the reader into the rot-
ting building with its corrupt face. The architect is no longer at work,
as his work no longer gracefully stands. And the "fair fables" or fairy
tales, or tales of goodness, fall or are no longer credible. This will not
be a story with a happy ending. None of the stories here have happy
endings. Gwendolyn is busy in this opening tercet. An additional in-
terpretation may present Gwendolyn in the traditional role of African
storyteller, or griot. An image is projected of black people gathering
around a fire, which provides the light that distorts faces. The back-
ground of the story is the ruin of the building and its builder. Finally,
when these fair fables fall, they are "fair" people's fables that fall. "Fair"
could be pale-complexioned people. Alternatively, if "fair" means just
or right, then the just fables fall. What is right and just does not occur.

Gwendolyn wanted to explore the misery, tensions, distortions, and hope that resided in the roach- and rat-infested building that had once been grand. The underlying idea is that human beings are born into an innate dignity, only to deteriorate from neglect and cruelty, as do the inhabitants of the Mecca.

The character Sallie Smith is a domestic worker like so many black women of that time. After work, she arrives home, ascends the "sick and influential stair," so like herself. She has eaten leftovers at work where white people have feasted on the food she prepared. She is plump and "low-brown," brown-skinned. In her weariness and slow letting go of the white world, she is "A fragmentary attar and armed coma / a fugitive attar and a district hymn." She is a lovely scent and a sleep walker, not fully aware of her own power. She eludes the understanding of others. She is a sacred song of a certain region of the city, the black region. Hence, white people cannot catch her soul or understand her entirely.

We also meet the ecstatically religious Saint Julia Jones, who is with a young and lecherous Prophet Williams, who caused his wife, Ida, to "die in self-defense." What is interesting to note as a rallying cry for black women, Gwendolyn addresses the audience ("Kinswomen! Kinswomen!") about the plight of Ida having "died alone." This should not be, says the poet; we are kin, of a tribe. Ida should have been supported, comforted, or even taken in by other black women.

Gwendolyn is also telling us that black women are her target audience or its better half. This is very important. It is the first time she had really announced her intended audience. Perhaps it is the first time that black people have been the sole intended audience for her work. The vocabulary of the appeal, "Kinswomen," suggests an African identification. Gwendolyn had moved considerably in her political awareness and tells us so in just two words in a long poem.

Mrs. Sallie Smith speaks to Saint Julia Jones and Prophet Williams and moves on; she does not linger. Hyena, a bleached-blond debutante, "to the tune of self-hate," bursts out of a doorway. The poet again announces her own shift in consciousness, making a judgment about the black woman who dyes her hair blond. Mrs. Sallie sees Alfred, an untalented writer who keeps writing while he teaches English, badly, at Wendell Phillips High School. "At faculty lunch hour / he allows the zoology teacher, who has great legs / to fondle him and curse his pretty hair." At night he sleeps with Telly Bell, a Meccan woman in 309, or with the Hyena. Alfred drinks, thinks, and reads an assortment of white, male literary masters. "So he is weak . . . It is a decent enough no-goodness."

A boy breaks glass and Mrs. Sallie
rises to the final and fourth floor.

Something is shattered as Mrs. Sallie reaches her destination. Some reflection has ended and some broken act is about to begin. It is a beginning that is an ending. It is the final floor as opposed to the highest.

The poet addresses Mrs. Sallie's children, and all of us who are the children of mothers who earn their bread by doing domestic work. She speaks to the collective. Mrs. Sallie has brought "hock of ham" and "mustard" (greens) cooked by an "Undaunted" eldest daughter "who once pushed her thumbs in the eyes of a Thief." Lastly, we children are given "six ruddy yams" and hot-water cornbread. It is the best that the mother can do. It is a traditional soul-food dinner.

Mrs. Sallie perches her hat on the kitchen table and surveys the "sick kitchen" thinking of all the changes she wants to make, but cannot afford to. It is no use. The environment is deeply wrong, and superficial decorations will not be enough. They would resemble "a pomade atop a sewage."

One of Mrs. Sallie's children, chewing gum, prepares to meet a boyfriend. This is Yvonne, the brave eldest. Most of the remaining children come into view one by one: Melodie Mary, Cap, Casey, Thomas Earl, Tennessee, Emmett, and Briggs. All of these young people "hate sewn suburbs," meaning white people and the accoutrements of white people, things that they do not have. Each child of Mrs. Sallie has his or her particularity and story. Melodie Mary likes or pities rats and roaches, ruminates on China. Reticent Briggs joins a gang. Tennessee wants to be like his contented cat. "Thomas Earl loves Johnny Appleseed." Emmett, Cap, and Casey are malnourished, in need of the soul food their mother prepares for them but does not always have enough of. They are not healthily fattened off treats.

Alfred, the failed writer and schoolteacher, considers Mrs. Sallie and her relationship to the "toy child" she cares for at work. Mrs. Sallie "evokes and loves and loathes pink lit image / of the toy child." There is a world of difference between what the world has for Mrs. Sallie's children and the "toy child," the white child. In summation, "What else is there to say but everything?" That everything includes aesthetics, politics, economics, history, sociology, psychology, anthropology, even culinary arts. When Mrs. Sallie considers the "toy child," she comes upon her own absent child.

Suddenly, realization comes in capital letters: "SUDDENLY, COUNTING NOSES, MRS. SALLIE / SEES NO PEPITA, 'WHERE PEPITA BE?'"

She queries each of her children on the whereabouts of Pepita. The mother is distraught. The children all chime that they "Ainseener" again and again. The children cut off their individual preoccupations and go from door to door throughout the building in search of Pepita. Gwendolyn captures the hysterical mood of the desperate search for the little girl.

We meet the neighbors as the search goes on: Great-great Gram remembers sleeping on a vermin-infested dirt floor during slavery; Loam Norton is Jewish and considers the concentration camp; Bootsie DeBroe is a Lady; John-Tom is the kind neighbor whose phone Emmett uses to call the police.

The police arrive but are in no hurry to help, but eventually they leave with a photo of Pepita and begin pounding on neighbors' doors. Aunt Dill also comes and causes greater worry with her tales of bad endings.

We encounter Alfred the schoolteacher again as he weaves a long story about Senghor, the Senegalese poet of Negritude who was president of Senegal. Hyena returns and speaks disdainfully of Pepita. She earns her animalistic name because she shows no genuine feeling. Mazola ruminates on Death and the body going out of a house. Then, all of a sudden, we are presented with Don Lee, an actual historical poet figure; Lee is spoken of with a sense of his fire and moral rectitude. He is refreshingly juxtaposed to Alfred, who is without talent, and he is juxtaposed to the terrible brokenness and depression of the Mecca. He is a "physical light," a living candle against the gloom in which there is no way to see, especially at this moment when a child is lost.

The character of Amos meditates on the need to cleanse America of her falsehood. The ballad of Edie Barrow is striking in its formalism. It has the feeling of being a part of an earlier version of *In the Mecca*. Edie loved a Gentile boy who married one of his own kind. There is also a lengthy consideration of Prophet Williams, who brings to mind the tricks that Gwendolyn observed while she worked for such a charlatan.

The poet asks, "How many care, Pepita?" She asks the lost child who would know, because the lost child would know who really cares for her. Then she offers a short roll call of names: Staley and Lara, Eunie, Simpson, Bixby and June. "Not those." They do not care. And the prostitutes do not care. These are the three Maries, whom it would seem are precursors to Toni Morrison's three Maries in *The Bluest Eye*. Great-uncle Beer is a sporting man; Wezlyn wanders the halls in her insane search for her lover, Lawrence; Wezlyn earns much space as she represents the madness of the place. The following also do not care about Pepita: Darkara (who looks at *Vogue*), Aunt Tippie, Zombie Bell, Mr. Kelly, Gas Cady, the grave robber of flowers, the political janitor, and Walace Williams.

Alfred appears again, to offer bad poetry. The policemen come upon the twins who put flour on their own faces, perhaps symbolic of their self-hate. Perhaps Gwendolyn is having fun with this extreme image. Way-Out Morgan collects guns to enact vengeance on white men who gave him "three local and legal beatings" and who "mob-raped" his sister in Mississippi. As a debt collector, he is like Morrison's

Seven Days in *Song of Solomon*. It is easy to imagine such a vengeful black character with a grudge against white people, but in reality, black people are rarely vengeful toward whites.

Marian is busy cooking, longing to be seen. And Aunt Dill, who appears again, is a woman of fake religiosity and pretense.

Alfred senses the greatness stirring in the Mecca in spite of it all.

The last quatrain of "In the Mecca" is a worrisome whisper that bothers the heart of the reader and continues past the first and second reading. It describes when Pepita is discovered, and we are told of the sounds she made as she died.

The collection *In the Mecca* is Gwendolyn's most artistically revolutionary work. It follows no formal pattern. It contains disruptions in typography as far as the sudden use of capitalization with "WHERE BE PEPITA" and the joining of words and sentences "ainseenher-ainseenher" to create a sense of panic, hysteria. With these effects, Gwendolyn places the reader in the scene and in a state of agitation if not terror.

The narrative itself is not continuous but told in disjointed stanzas, just as the people in the Mecca dwell in a state of disjointedness. They live their separate existences in their separate apartments. They lack a sense of community and unity, which Gwendolyn would later more openly accuse black people of lacking.

As in no other of her works, Gwendolyn presides over this long poem as a loving, stern, and authoritative presence. She is as "unapologetically Black" as the *Chicago Defender* says it is. She is not afraid to make value judgments or directly address her black audience, unlike in her previous work.

The poems of *After Mecca* are as memorable as the extended work. In this suite were published a number of Gwendolyn's most iconic poems, those that provide a broad context for the long narrative, but with many sounding the positive resonances of the Black Consciousness movement. They reflect most clearly Gwendolyn's own state of mind, her psychological transformation from Negro to black woman.

The after-set begins with "To a Winter Squirrel," in which Merdice, so named to suggest her own "murdered heart," is "cleaning guts," chitterlings, at the kitchen window and observing a squirrel outside. Notes for the poem came to Gwendolyn while she cleaned chitterlings, which she was taught to prepare by Gloria Bennett, wife of Lerone and a longtime friend. Merdice, in her cold house heated by a stove, as her "landlord has no coal," considers the squirrel with delight and admiration. She admires its self-sufficiency and pleasure in itself. Just as Merdice delights in these things, it is easy to imagine Gwendolyn delighting in these qualities, as she had delighted in the young black people she met in the late 1960s and their self-possession.

Medgar Evers was the field secretary of the NAACP in Mississippi. He led the fight to end segregation at the University of Mississippi and the fight for economic justice and voting rights, and worked to end American apartheid in public facilities. He eloquently stated, "You can kill a man, but you can't kill an idea." He was murdered by Byron De La Beckwith on June 12, 1963, shot in his own driveway as he arrived home early that morning after work. He was rushed to the hospital where they refused him medical attention. When they were told who he was, the hospital finally admitted him, but Evers died less than an hour later. His assassination sparked outrage. De La Beckwith was tried and acquitted twice, but was finally found guilty in 1994. Gwendolyn was one of several writers who praised Evers, along with James Baldwin, Eudora Welty, and Gwendolyn's friend Margaret Walker.

"Medgar Evers" begins with this quatrain:

The man whose height his fear improved he
arranged to fear no further. The raw
intoxicated time was time for better birth or
a final death.

Gwendolyn has in these four lines the ability to see into a human question—How does overcoming fear in the face of a desired end make us better human beings? We have to choose to be better even if it means that we will die. This is a stunning assertion. It is a revolutionary announcement. Again, she considers the importance of the quality of courage.

The last tercet holds the result of Evers's courageous quest:

Roaring no rapt arise-ye to the dead, he
leaned across tomorrow. People said that
he was holding clean globes in his hands.

Evers did not make a great noise to raise the dead. He simply evoked the future by his deliberate actions. It is significant that he was holding clean globes as if his actions had cleansed two worlds. Those worlds, separate and equal, black and white, are now clean by his sacrifice. Additional poems in the "After Mecca" section include those derived from Gwendolyn's experiences with the Blackstone Rangers street gang. These poems prove profoundly ambivalent and ambiguous about the Rangers, who some see as "Sores in the city / that do not want to heal." Yet "construct strangely, a monstrous pearl or grace." She admonishes girls in gangs, "A Rangerette" to "settle for sandwiches! Settle for stocking caps! . . . the props and niceties of non-loneliness." She advises the Rangerette, Mary, to seek a more conventional union, a safer life. Gwendolyn had not prejudged the Blackstone Rangers and Rangerettes. She got to know them and offered them respect and assistance in self-expression. In these poems, she offers readers a chance to experience them too.

In the two "Sermons on the Warpland," for the first time Gwendolyn chooses to speak as a prophet. The poet and critic Larry Neal had exhorted black poets to function as priests and prophets. Gwendolyn was reluctant to envision herself in this exalted role, but when she elevated her voice and made her diction grander, she achieved an authority to advise the masses. The Warpland is America as designated by this prophet, a twisted land, a perverted land. This is strong language, but Gwendolyn declines to portray herself as the prophet she is. "They're little addresses to Black people, that's all."[10]

The first sermon, not as well known as the second sermon on the Warpland, opens with an epigram from Ron Karenga, social scientist, cultural nationalist, and founder of Kwanzaa: "The fact that we are black is our ultimate reality."

And several strengths from drowsiness campaigned
but spoke in Single Sermon upon the warpland.

And went about the warpland saying No.
"My people, black and black, revile the River.
Say that the River turns, and turn the River.

Say that our Something in doublepod contains
seeds for the coming hell and health together.
Prepare to meet
(sisters, brothers) the brash and terrible weather;
the pains;
the bruising; the collapse of bestials, idols.
But then oh then!—the stuffing of the hulls!
the seasoning of the perilously sweet!
the health! The heralding of the clear obscure!

Build now your Church, my brothers, sisters. Build
never with brick or Corten nor with granite.
Build with lithe love. With love like lion-eyes.
with love like morningrise.
with love like black, our black—
luminously indiscreet;
complete; continuous."

Gwendolyn personifies the Black Consciousness/Black Power/ Black Art movements as one who has awakened and mounted a campaign marked by No. These movements must say no to the status quo, no to white supremacy, white standards of beauty, white hegemony, economic disparity, disparity of opportunity, and overall social in-equality. At the root of the status quo is the belief in black subhu-manity and in black aesthetic and intellectual inferiority. The Black Consciousness/Black Power/Black Art movements said no to these myths and yes to the concepts of "Black Is Beautiful," a black heritage of excellence, black self-definition, black self-determination, black pride, and black unity.

Gwendolyn, speaking as "the strengths," admonishes her black community that our specialness in union with one another makes us able to meet whatever is to come. Prepare for the worst, she warns, for it is coming. Old idols will be torn down. Those "bestials" who mistreat us will be overthrown. Even those we erected, as the Hebrews erected the golden calf on their way to the Promised Land, will be overthrown. It will be a rich, fulfilling time for black people, a time of health, celebration, and clarity. In the meantime, it is important that we build up our black community. Nothing is stronger or more beautiful than love among the whole black community.

That is the bare-bones message of the prophetic poem. Its spiritual message and uplifting quality are in the heightened language and the lyricism that is almost songlike, mesmerizing. There is such a thing as grace. "The Sermon on the Warpland" has the compelling, lyrical pull of the Beatitudes. It also offers a firm spiritual lesson. It is worthy to be used to make Church. Gwendolyn conjoins religion and politics through the vehicle of black love and unity.

She also believed in the unity of word and deed: first, "revile the River," denounce what is going on; then "Say that the River turns," that is, say that what is going on is moving in a new direction; fi-nally, "turn the River," turn the course of events yourself. In this poem Gwendolyn laid a course for herself.

One poem in the collection is significant not only for its beauty but also for its historical significance. Hoyt W. Fuller at *Negro Digest* wrote to Gwendolyn, "What a marvelous poem, 'The Wall!' My word, it made me tingle!"[11]

THE WALL
   August 27, 1967
   For Edward Christmas

"The side wall of a typical slum building on the corner of 43rd
and Langley became a mural communicating black dignity . . ."
                                                              —*Ebony*

     A drumdrumdrum
     Humbly we come.
South of success and east of gloss and glass are
sandals;
flowercloth;
grave hoops of wood or gold, pendant
from black ears, brown ears, reddish-brown
and ivory ears;

black boy-men
Black
boy-men on roofs fist out "Black Power!" Val,
a little black stampede
in African images of brass and flowerswirl,

fists out "Black Power!"—tightens pretty eyes,
leans back on mothercountry and is tract,
is treatise through her perfect and tight teeth.

Women in wool hair chant their poetry.
Phil Cohran gives us messages and music
made of developed bone and polished and honed
          cult.
It is the Hour of tribe and of vibration,
the day-long Hour. It is the Hour
of ringing, rouse, of ferment-festival.

On Forty-third and Langley
black furnaces resent ancient
legislatures
of ploy and scruple and practical gelatin.
They keep the fever in,
fondle the fever.

All
worship the Wall.

I mount the rattling wood. Walter
says, "She is good." Says, "She
our Sister is." In front of me
hundreds of faces, red-brown, brown, black, ivory,
yield me hot trust, their yea and their
      Announcement
that they are ready to rile the high-flung ground.
Behind me. Paint.
Heroes.
No child has defiled.
the Heroes of this Wall this serious Appointment
this still Wing
this Scald this Flute this heavy Light this Hinge.

An emphasis is paroled.
The old decapitations are revised,
the dispossessions beakless.

And we sing.

Thus commemorates the inauguration of the Wall of Respect, the 1967 mural, and Gwendolyn's own re-initiation into the black community as a black woman of African-identified consciousness and rallied social consciousness. "The Wall" is also a celebration of the diversity of the Afro-American community in all its colors and shades, a description of the black community in full embrace of itself and its heroes. The wall itself is a place where the people might take flight, be burned blacker, lured, illuminated, and given entrance to another, more glorious reality of healing.

After the dedication ceremony had concluded, the poets moved their feast of black poetry to a nearby neighborhood tavern, the Playboy Lounge. The OBAC poets in their African garb paraded into the lounge. They were friendly and down to earth. Hoyt W. Fuller, Gwendolyn, and the OBAC writers merged with the other patrons. Soon someone from OBAC said,

> "Say, folks, we're going to lay some poetry on you!" Gwendolyn said, "I wondered how they were going to respond to poetry. The poets started reading, and before we knew it, people had turned around on their bar stools, with their drinks behind them, and were listening. Then they applauded. And I thought that was a wonderful thing, something new. I want to write poetry—and it won't be Ezra Pound poetry, as you can imagine—that will be exciting to such people. And I don't see why it can't be 'good' poetry," putting quotes around "good."[12]

The day of the Wall of Respect and the reading at the Playboy Lounge, and the delivery of *In the Mecca* soon thereafter to Harper & Row, mark a signal period in the life of the poet. *In the Mecca* would be the last book of new work that Gwendolyn would publish with a white publisher. It marked an artistic high point, although it was not universally glowingly received. It lives well, however. And it carried Gwendolyn into a newer, blacker time as a woman and as an artist.

CHAPTER SEVEN

A Surprised Queenhood

In her 1972 autobiography, *Report from Part One*, Gwendolyn Brooks wrote:

> I—who have "gone the gamut" from an almost angry rejection of my dark skin by some of my brainwashed brothers and sisters to a surprised queenhood in the new black sun—am qualified to enter at least the kindergarten of new consciousness now. New consciousness and trudge—toward—progress.
>
> I have hopes for myself.

Gwendolyn was further along toward her queenhood, and further than in a kindergarten of black consciousness, further than she herself knew. After all, she was a favorite daughter of the Negro community and had achieved the status of an icon when in 1950 she became the first black person to be awarded a Pulitzer Prize.

Throughout the 1950s, she did not travel much and gave a limited number of readings, but by the 1960s, as her daughter, Nora, grew older, Gwendolyn became a regular presenter of her works in Chicago public schools, from Copernicus to Tanner, down the street from her house. She had a special way with children, who loved her expressive style and her ease with them. She was Somebody, and they knew it.

In 1962, she and Langston Hughes were the only Negro poets to read at the National Poetry Festival, sponsored by the Library of Congress. In 1965, the Metropolitan Community Church honored her at a testimonial at the Pick-Congress Hotel, in downtown Chicago. She was royalty, of a kind.

It was the young black people who had ignited the fires that smoldered in her, the young black poets who had put the light in her eyes. A new world beckoned.

Even before the Fisk Writers Conference of April 1967, in February 1966, she had given a reading in Rochester, Michigan, and met another poet who would be important on her path to the new Black Consciousness. Dudley Randall struck her as a gentle man, not at all as she had anticipated from his tough reviews in *Negro Digest*. "Oh, you're Dudley Randall. I thought you were terrible, but you're all right," he remembered her saying.[1] They had dinner at his house, with his wife, and poets Oliver LaGrone, Joyce Whitsit, and Harold Lawrence. Randall was a longtime admirer of Gwendolyn's poetry and asked her to contribute to his publishing house.

Broadside Press was born when Randall published his own civil rights poem, "Ballad of Birmingham." He asked Gwendolyn if he might do broadsides of her poems "We Real Cool" and "Martin Luther King Jr." Soon, Randall and Margaret Burroughs were editing an anthology dedicated to Malcolm X. Gwendolyn sent her legendary poem "Malcolm X" for what would become *Malcolm: Poems on the Life and Death of Malcolm*, published in May 1967.

In 1968, Don Lee was published through Broadside Press. He had been recommended by Margaret Burroughs after self-publishing *Think Black*. Broadside Press published *Black Pride*, then the blockbuster and artistically ground-breaking *Don't Cry, Scream*. Lee was satisfied with his publisher and wanted to contribute even more to the development of the black community. He knew that Gwendolyn had reached the point in her political sentiments that she was ready to move from Harper & Row. He influenced her to publish her new work at Broadside Press.

Gwendolyn listened and agreed. But make no mistake about it—she put her work where she professed that it should be. She expressed black unity and fidelity to black economic prosperity and the liberation of black psyches. She believed that she had to build up a black publishing house. It was, she believed, her duty. Lee stressed to her the importance of institution building, of building black schools, publishing houses, and organizations that would live beyond the lifespans of their founders. This business of institution building was central to the thinking of the Black Arts Movement in Chicago which, as it turns out, would prove to be the intellectual center of the movement. Gwendolyn was in the thick of things.

In 1968 and 1969, she and Lee often gave readings together across the country. In the beginning, she would read from her work and then introduce the younger poet to the audience. Lee was a dynamic reader and did not disappoint Gwendolyn's faith in him. She was acting as a poetic mentor. After a time, Lee became dissatisfied with the order of their readings. He found her reading before him disrespectful of her as the elder, more esteemed poet. He insisted on reading first and presenting her. She was, after all, Gwendolyn Brooks, a kind of mother to a group of younger black poets, particularly Lee and Walter Bradford.

Ann McNeil, now Dr. Ann Smith, met Gwendolyn Brooks at Northeastern Illinois State College in the fall of 1966. They had "cubbies," cubicles, close to each other. Gwendolyn was teaching in the English Department; she had a title of some distinction—Distinguished Lecturer—but no official trappings, not even an office. Smith was familiar with Gwendolyn, of course, from her writings. As a professor and an actor in the Speech and Theater Department, Smith was well versed in black literature, and Gwendolyn was a key figure. In person, Smith noticed that Gwendolyn was "quiet, unassuming, intentionally shy. She didn't reach out to be the center of attention, even when she was. She did not seek the limelight."

As their friendship developed, Smith found Gwendolyn had a sense of humor and that "her conversation was like her poetry. She didn't waste words. She was self-deprecating and very kind." Smith remembers Gwendolyn's deceptive simplicity, even her "simplicity in attire. … People would say that she was stand-offish, but in fact, she was shy." In truth, Gwendolyn was shy, but she could be stand-offish, too.

When Smith first met Gwendolyn, neither was involved in any black groups. But in 1967, Smith met Hoyt W. Fuller and became involved with OBAC. That same year, Gwendolyn took a different route to become involved with some of the same people. By the spring of 1968, Smith knew Gwendolyn better through her involvement with a special celebration of her work at Northeastern Illinois. At that program, Smith performed Gwendolyn's poem "the mother," and Jeff Donaldson, OBAC visual artist and actor, presented her "of DeWitt Williams on his way to Lincoln Cemetery."

Gwendolyn would list Dr. Smith in her inner circle. This relationship expanded the shy poet's circle within the Black Arts community. But she had always been a part of Chicago, even if she had always considered herself somewhat of a loner. In May 1965 when it was reported that Chicago had paid homage to Gwendolyn, it was also reported that she had paid homage to Chicago. "Asking me why I like Chicago is like asking me why I like my blood."[2] She had never been called the poet of Chicago but said it would be a great honor if she was.

By January of 1968, homage to Gwendolyn would be institutionalized statewide when she succeeded Carl Sandburg as the poet laureate of Illinois. Of this appointment, Gwendolyn said, "Being the state's poet laureate is an honor for which I will receive no pay. … And that's only fair because right now, I don't plan to write any poems."[3] But she managed to write beautiful poems as laureate, most notably, "Aurora," which she wrote in January 1973 for the inauguration of Governor Dan Walker.

> *We who are weak and wonderful*
> *wicked, bewildered, wistful and wild*
> *are saying direct good morning*

through the fever
  It is the giant-hour,
Nothing less than gianthood will do;
nothing less than mover, prover,
shover, cover, lever, diver
for giant tacklings, overturning new
organic staring,
that will involve that will involve us
all.
  We say direct good-morning
through the fever,
across the brooding obliques, the
somersaults, ashes
across
the importances stylishly killed:
across
the edited bias,
the waffling of woman,
the structured rejection of blackness.
  Ready for ways,
windows,
remodeling spirals; closing the hot
clichés
Unwinding the witchcraft.
  Opening to sun.

This is the Gwendolyn Brooks of mysterious language as in *Annie Allen*. She is poet laureate and a bit studied, beautifully. (We will look more closely at "Aurora" later.)

In the early 1960s, Gwendolyn had begun giving literary prizes to pupils at various Chicago public schools. These prizes were small (twenty-five dollars) but significant to the children who received them. When Gwendolyn was designated poet laureate of Illinois, she was determined to make her title meaningful and not just decorative or utilitarian—writing occasionally for the erection of buildings or the births of corporations or the inaugurations of public officers. She felt that a poet laureate should do more than "wear a crown" and "should be of service to the young." To this end, she instituted two annual awards of $250 each for poetry by Illinois residents. The first awards were given in May 1970 by judges Hoyt W. Fuller and the poet Paul Carroll. The winners were from Chicago and Morton Grove respectively. The former wrote a poem called "Black" and the latter, a poem titled "Tranquility Broken." It would appear that one of the young poets was black and the other white. Gwendolyn recognized all talent. In 1972 she increased her giving by adding a $100 prize to a runner-up. The Illinois Arts Council matched her gift with another $100 for a runner-up.

Also in 1972, Gwendolyn gave money to an OBAC writers' workshop poetry contest held at the Center for Inner City Studies, where she established a $100 first prize, a $50 second prize, and a $25 third prize for poets. The judges were Ronda Davis of OBAC and the Gwendolyn Brooks Workshop, Sterling Plumpp, Andrew Wasaiah, and Angela Jackson. The children and their teacher, Mrs. Virginia Johnson, were exuberant. The children were spruced up and buoyant in their presentations. They were black and proud. One of them, Rhinold Ponder, is a poet still, and a lawyer. Sterling Plumpp also gave ten dollars of his own to a number of honorable mentions. Gwendolyn's generosity inspired generosity in others.

Gwendolyn's commitment to the black community had sparked in her a pattern of giving. In 1970, she initiated the Gwendolyn Brooks Literary Awards through *Black World* magazine (formerly *Negro Digest*). The first award, to poet Brenda Torres, was for $500. The next year, Maye Boyes Sanders received $250 for fiction, and Garfield Jackson received $250 for poetry.

In summer of 1969, Gwendolyn gave four thousand dollars to send two young black writers to Africa for their enrichment. It pleased her to impact their lives in this way. She gave freely to those in need. Some worried that people would take advantage of her goodness, but others who knew her better knew that she was not naïve. Gwendolyn understood that in giving, we receive. Even today, she symbolizes a model of public and private generosity for artists and citizens.

Having sent two young black writers on a trip to Africa at her own expense, in 1971, she felt it was time for her to go. She made plans to journey with Don Lee to East Africa—Kenya and Tanzania. These were nations where the people spoke Kiswahili and English as well. They welcomed black Americans. Tanzania, especially, was of interest to black Americans of Black Consciousness because its president, Julius Nyerere, was a proponent of African socialism, Ujamaa, the collective economic development of the nation to benefit all the people and not just a few, as in a capitalistic mode of development. Nyerere's ideas were appealing to people like Lee, who wanted to see Tanzania for himself, to be a part of its progress. Gwendolyn also wanted to see the emerging nation and the beauty of the homeland.

She made preparations with her cultural "son," but his plans were curtailed by a family emergency. Gwendolyn would have to set out alone. Lee was worried. In July, he wrote to her, "As you travel it may be best that you drink *bottled* water. Be careful with your meat and try to mainly eat fruits or vegetables." He directed her to a friend in Tanzania, the poet Charlie Cobb. Of him Lee said, "You can trust him as you trust *me*. He's a true brother."[4]

There was an urgency to Gwendolyn's journey to Africa. She believed that her primary focus and the focus of all black people should be on black unity. She believed it was the compelling duty of black people worldwide to operate in the economic and social interest of all black people. She did not warm to the popular concept of Third World unity. She was devoted to Black Familyhood, Black Community, and Black World.

She arrived in Nairobi with high hopes and a feeling of familiarity. The Kenyans, of course, saw her as an Afro-American, not a long-lost sister or cousin.

After settling in at the expensive Panafric Hotel, Gwendolyn set out on foot to find a store to purchase snacks. As was her way, she observed the life of the people on the street, the music of their speech, the buoyancy of their walk. She felt a fierce desire to belong, a regret that she and her tribe, black Americans, did not belong on the homeland. She felt resentment toward the white restaurant manager who was boss to the servers. He called them "boy." Gwendolyn thought "slave." The implications of a history of kidnapping, colonization, and enslavement embittered her, even as she was seized by the sweetness of being in Africa.

Even in the small neighborhood store, she questioned the presence of the Indian woman storekeeper who came from somewhere else and had the right to sell her wafers, sardines, and cans of orange juice. Gwendolyn tried to learn the system of money. She brooded on the history of human trade that had left her with no African language and her African relatives with only recent rights to their own land, but no clear ownership.

She was able to obtain a meeting with the mayor of Nairobi. Her friend Era Bell Thompson, international editor of *Ebony* magazine, had written a letter to the mayor, Margaret Kenyatta, but the letter did not even arrive until Gwendolyn was back in Chicago. Even so, Kenyatta, daughter of the famed Jomo Kenyatta, liberator of Kenya, graciously received Gwendolyn even though she was quite busy and did not, it would seem, fully appreciate who Gwendolyn Brooks was. She was not fully aware of her reputation as the premiere Afro-American poet and one of America's most esteemed poets. Gwendolyn, after all, was a quiet woman, simply dressed and not ostentatious. And what is a poet to a politician of another country?

Formally, the mayor offered Gwendolyn coffee. There was a ritual surrounding the serving of coffee that was very important. When Gwendolyn initially declined the offering, Kenyatta's secretary was crestfallen. Gwendolyn quickly changed her mind and accepted. She chatted formally with Kenyatta about Era Bell Thompson and her well-being, workload, and writing.

If Mayor Kenyatta had received the letter of introduction, it would have been an ice-breaker. Gwendolyn was offered more coffee. She asked if she might tour the University of Nairobi. Miss Kenyatta made phone calls to make this happen. When talk turned to poetry, the mayor expressed her preference for Okot p'Bitek, the Ugandan poet who wrote "Song of Lawino," a poem in the voice of a traditional wife who represents the traditional ways of the people. Gwendolyn had found the book-length poem delightfully admirable. Her admiration pleased the mayor.

Nora had taken a six-week course at the University of Nairobi the year before Gwendolyn's visit, so Gwendolyn had some idea of what to expect. She people-watched as she sat in the Education building—white professors, easy-limbed and easygoing Kenyan students with close-cropped hair, Afro-Americans with big naturals. She went to the gift shop and haggled with the marketer as Nora had instructed her. All the while, the regret that she knew no African tongue lingered with her. She was a master of English, but no more than an infant in any language of her ancestral land.

As she was leaving Kenya, the Kikuyu driver told her that if they had known in time that she was coming, arrangements could have been made for her to visit homes or even stay in one. If she had known, she could have selected a less expensive hotel that was just as nice. Perhaps the servers who seemed to hurry her through her meal were used to European travelers and did not quite know what to do with this simply-dressed black woman with the unassuming demeanor. She was no Ugly American. And yet, she was not a Continental African.

In 1974, when the Sixth Pan-African Congress was held in Dar es Salaam, the population of Afro-Americans in Tanzania was seven hundred to eight hundred. This was when black revolutionaries of every persuasion—including Black Panthers, cultural nationalists, Pan-Africanists, and Garveyites—sought refuge in Tanzania, the epicenter of activity for Afro-Americans of consciousness. This lasted until 1974, when a misunderstanding over several undeclared weapons in customs exacerbated relations between the Tanzanian government and black Americans.[5] Until that time, black Americans had enjoyed a great sense of community in the East African nation. When

Gwendolyn Brooks visited Dar es Salaam, it was as its name said, City of Peace, and her stay there was peaceful, even warm and welcoming.

Her experience in Tanzania was quite different from her time in Kenya. It was not marked by the formality of her meeting with Mayor Margaret Kenyatta. In Tanzania, she was among friends—or friends of friends. She stayed at the home of Charlie and Gayleatha Cobb. She had met Charlie before, as Don Lee had brought him to meet her when Cobb was in Chicago. Now Cobb was in Africa, and his wife was just starting to work at the University of Dar es Salaam.

They lived in a German-style stone house on wide, expansive grounds. As was the custom of professionals, they had household help from an African couple with markings on their faces. Gwendolyn noticed these people and accepted their welcome. Her days spent at the Cobbs' home were spent in hospitality. She found joy in cooking for her hosts, preparing American food after going to the market daily and shopping with her basket. She fixed lamb chops or corned beef with vegetables and light desserts. It is charming to imagine Gwendolyn traveling around the world to perform the womanly task of cooking that she had done for her family for so many years. It suggests that for her, cooking, as well as writing, were acts of love and tender and precise service.

With the Cobbs, she visited other Afro-Americans, trading stories, memories, a world of ideas, for these expatriates were educated men and women with strong and well-thought-out opinions. They explained to Gwendolyn, the visitor, how American black people had to be ready for differences when they came to Africa. Americans were impatient or wanted things done immediately. Africans adopted an attitude of patience, as it took a while to get certain things done. Materials were not always readily at hand and had to be shipped sometimes from another continent. Gwendolyn's new friends laughed at how Africans were cautious of black Americans and their incendiary ideas. Ultimately, and unfortunately, this fear of Afro-Americans would cause a large number of black Americans to leave Tanzania. But that was to come later. While Gwendolyn was in Tanzania, she found pleasure, giving a reading at the Teacher's College and meeting with the legendary West African novelist Ayi Kwei Armah and other Afro-Americans in that community, a long way from their American "home."

She was a black woman of Pan-African sensibility, a woman of single consciousness, as she had come to know a few years before. She no longer suffered that "double-consciousness" that W. E. B. Du Bois described in *The Souls of Black Folk* in 1903:

> It is a peculiar sensation, this double-consciousness, this sense of always looking at one's self through the eyes of others, of measuring one's soul by the tape of a world that looks on in amused contempt and pity. One ever feels his two-ness, an American, a Negro; two souls, two unreconciled strivings; two warring ideals in one dark body, whose dogged strength alone keeps it from being torn asunder. The history of the American Negro is the history of this strife—the longing to attain self-conscious manhood, to merge his double-self into a better and truer self. In this merging he wishes neither of the older selves to be lost. He does not wish to Africanize America, for America has too much to teach the world and Africa. He wouldn't bleach his Negro blood in a flood of white Americanism, for he knows that Negro blood has a message to the world. He simply wishes to make it possible for a man to be both a Negro and an American without being cursed and spit upon by his fellows, without having the doors opportunity closed roughly in his face.[6]

Only Gwendolyn, at this point, was not so consciously interested in adhering to the American identity. She had undergone, in a short time, changes at a profound psychological level. It was a change in her idea of identity. Even though she carefully, maternally, prepared American food, she was asserting her Africanness in every way. Her American self had been carved through a veil of tears, sweat, and blood. She was "essentially an essential African."[7] She was interested in her black consciousness and professing the single-mindedness of that in her writing. That single consciousness evolved from that epiphany when the Wall of Respect was dedicated and the OBAC poets took over the Playboy Tavern with their black poetry for black people. She wanted to do the same—seek out all black people with her words. She had a new poetic imperative.

She presented Broadside Press with *Riot*, a small volume containing one long poem about events following the assassination of Martin Luther King Jr.

Riot was published in 1969. It is the first volume that Gwendolyn published with an independent black press. This was a brave act; to a certain extent, it was self-sacrificial because Broadside Press did not have the production or advertising budget of Harper & Row. Gwendolyn took the risk of leaving a good portion of her reputation behind, but she put her faith in people who believed in black people, black pride, and black independence, and she welcomed the change.

Riot is in three parts. The first is a portrait of the wealthy, white suburbanite John Cabot; the second is the "Third Sermon on the Warpland," a diffused description of the riot in Chicago the day after King's assassination; and the third is the love poem, "An Aspect of Love, Alive in the Ice and Fire." John Cabot is a male counterpart to the women in the poem "Lovers of the Poor" from *The Bean Eaters*. In keeping with her new mission to create work that was available to the masses of black people, the poem "Riot" is written in a more direct diction. Thus Cabot's aversion to "the Negroes" is unadorned. He does not mince words.

RIOT

John Cabot, out of Wilma, once a Wycliffe,
all whitebluerose below his golden hair,
wrapped richly in right linen and right wool,
almost forgot his Jaguar and Lake Bluff;
almost forgot Grandtully (which is The
Best Thing That Ever Happened to Scotch); almost

forgot the sculpture at the Richard Gray
and Distelheim; the kidney pie at Maxim's,
the Grenadine de Beouf at Maison Henri.

Because the "Negroes" were coming down the street.

Because the Poor were sweaty and unpretty
(not like Two Dainty Negroes in Winnetka)
and they were coming toward him in rough ranks.
In seas. In windsweep. They were black and loud.
And not detainable. And not discreet.

Gross. Gross. "Que tu es grossier!" John Cabot
itched instantly beneath the nourished white
that told his story of glory to the World.
"Don't let it touch me! The blackness! Lord!" he
whispered to any handy angel in the sky.

But, in a thrilling announcement, on It drove
and breathed on him; and touched him. In that breath
the fume of pig foot, chitterling and cheap chili,
malign, mocked John. And, in terrific touch, old
averted doubt jerked forward decently,
cried "Cabot! John! You are a desperate man,
and the desperate die expensively today."

John Cabot went down in the smoke and fire
and broken glass and blood, and he cried "Lord!
Forgive these nigguhs that know not what they do."

Even though Gwendolyn had moved to a cleaner, more direct style here, there is still much to engage and re-engage the reader. She is not talking down to a broad spectrum of black people. She begins with John Cabot's pedigree and uses brand names as connotations of wealth, for even if the brand is not familiar to her audience, then the name itself sounds rich. She cleverly questions the cultural superiority of Cabot's world to the black experience. Is kidney pie any better than chitterlings or chili? She makes fun of John Cabot in an obvious way, more overtly than in "Lovers of the Poor," in which the satire was more elaborate and understated.

For example, most readers would have some familiarity with Jesus's words on the cross: "Father, forgive them, for they know not what they do." Gwendolyn's people, as a rule, are familiar with the infinite mercy of Jesus Christ. She contrasts this well-known line with John Cabot's pompous pseudo-mercy laced with the racist epithet. The meaning of the final sentence would be hard to miss. The audience of black people is vindicated as Cabot receives his just deserts. He is overwhelmed by a sea of blackness. Gwendolyn's audience can forgive her casual display of French in the poem, and they can figure it out. She in no way identifies with John Cabot. She judges him.

After *Riot* was published, Gwendolyn became more involved with Broadside Press, recommending poets who should be published by it and using her own money to support these publications. She saw herself as a member of a kind of triumvirate of black publishing with Don Lee and Dudley Randall. She respected and admired them for their commitment to black people, their art, and the way in which they got things done. She was not a rich woman and never would be, but she had some resources, and she offered what she could to her community, which she had increasingly come to regard as family.

Her next volume of poetry, *Family Pictures*, appeared through Broadside Press in 1970. The highlight of the volume was the poem version of "The Life of Lincoln West." It was a piece she had labored on for decades, having already published it in short-story form. She felt an urgent need to speak the truth of a young black child disdained because of his or her color and features. She had to address the concept of aesthetics and had been wise enough to recognize its importance for many years. Now the Black Liberation and Black Arts movements were catching up to her. She had to bring

"Lincoln West" to the fore, for as she said at the Fisk conference, she was a Lincoln West.

The opening is brutal, but for some reason black audiences laughed.

Ugliest little boy
that everyone ever saw.
That is what everyone said.

Even to his mother it was apparent—

Lincoln West is described as having "The pendulous lip, the / branching ears, the eyes so wide and wild, / The vague unvibrant brown of the skin, / and, most disturbing, the great head." These features provided that the boy was most assuredly ugly. He was shunned and neglected by his mother, ignored by his father. When his teacher was momentarily kind to him, she regretted it. He clutched her hand as they walked down the street. People saw her with him. Lincoln's life was one of rejection or indignation from relatives who were angry because he was. The new neighborhood children liked his personality and his inventiveness with games until "nicer looking" playmates came around. "What a pity what a pity. No love / for one so loving."

Lincoln West lived with the absence of requited love until one day when he was seven, something happened.

a thing happened. In the down-town movies
with his mother a white
man in the seat beside him whispered
loudly to a companion, and pointed at
the little Linc.
"THERE! That's the kind I've been wanting
to show you! One of the best
examples of the specie. Not like
those diluted Negroes you see so much of on

the streets these days, but the
real thing.

Black, ugly, and odd. You
can see the savagery. The blunt
blankness. That is the real
thing."

One would think that little Lincoln would have been further in-
jured by being called "the real thing"—black, ugly, and odd. But,
heartbreakingly, Lincoln was used to being perceived as and called
ugly, and most importantly treated in an ugly way because "ugly" peo-
ple are treated in a less than loving way. Instead of being hurt again
little Lincoln meditated on being called "the real thing"; he was com-
forted by being found real or genuine. There is value in what is real,
as a diamond is worth more than cut glass. Lincoln was old enough
to grasp the concept. To be found real and admirable by anyone made
him happy. He felt validated in a way he did not around those who
ignored him, were angry at him, or neglected him.

"The Life of Lincoln West" is an excruciating poem, almost cruel in
its honesty, but it is successful because Gwendolyn, master that she is,
is able to present a difficult question of aesthetics and our response to
ideas of beauty with a delicate, comedic touch. The poem is humorous
and makes us laugh. Gwendolyn, the mother, feeds her black audience
the medicine of the truth about colorism with the honey of laughter.

The "Young Heroes" section of *Family Pictures* is handled with
straightforward seriousness. The three young men she salutes are all
poets to whom she feels connected: Keorapetse Kgositsile, Don Lee
(later Haki Madhubuti), and Walter Bradford. The first is a South
African poet in exile, affectionately called Willie.

TO KEORAPETSE KGOSITSILE (WILLIE)
He is very busy with his looking.
To look, he knows, is to involve

subject and suppliant.
He looks at life—
Moves life into his hands—
saying
Art is life worked with: is life
wheedled, or whelmed:
assessed:
clandestine, but evoked.
Look! Look to this page!
A horror here
walks toward you in working clothes.
Willie sees
hellishness among the half-men.
He sees
lenient dignity. He
sees pretty flowers under blood.
He teaches dolls and dynamite.
Because he knows
there is a scientific thinning of our ranks.
Not merely Medgar Malcolm Martin and Black Panthers,
But Susie. Cecil Williams. Azzie Jane.
He teaches
strategy and the straight aim;
Black volume;
might of mind, Black flare—
volcanoing merit, Black
herohood.

Black total.
    He is no kitten Traveler.
and no poor knower of himself.

    Blackness
is a going to essences and to unifyings.

"MY NAME IS AFRIKA!"
Well, every fella's a Foreign Country.

This Foreign Country speaks to You.

A gifted poet of diminutive stature like a stick of dynamite, Kgositsile brought the South African struggle home to Afro-Americans. He helped us understand the heavily armed white force that held apartheid in place over an overwhelming black majority. Willie brought this international nature of community home to Gwendolyn in a very personal way before she traveled to Africa. Through him, Gwendolyn understood that black familyhood was global.

In this poem, she captures the revolutionary young poet's ability to see with intelligence. He understands what he is looking at. He looks as an artist does, with subtlety perceiving and shaping perceptions. By writing these things down, he makes us see the evil that is done against our people, the massacres of many, not just the famously assassinated but ordinary black folk, "drylongso." He teaches us to respond with unity, intelligence, strategies of strength. He is not a simple tourist in America. He is a unifier. Gwendolyn says all of these things. Kgositsile says, "My Name Is Afrika," and Gwendolyn salutes him back. She tells us he is Afrika, and a foreign country. To be sure, Africa is a continent. Either she is simply geographically wrong or she is telling us that we must see Africa as one country, a unified Africa. Our strength lies in Pan-Africanism.

Of Lee, she paints a picture of an intense young black man in a casual moment, at ease from his work in the world. "I like to see you living in the world," she concludes. She is pleased with this cultural son of hers.

To her fellow Gemini cultural son Walter Bradford, she offers words of faith and encouragement: "it's a wilderness, Walter" . . . "It's Walter-Work, Walter." . . . "Not overmuch for a / Tree-planting Man." "Stay."

Finally, in "Young Afrikans," she applauds those "Who take Today and jerk it out of joint . . ." She pushes us to face the new time and to change the world with our hands and "hot blood." She herself is making changes. She follows the revolutionary Afrikan way of spelling "Africa"; she is at the forefront of change.

Gwendolyn had unfinished business with her former publisher. She was leaving Harper & Row behind with *The World of Gwendolyn Brooks*, published in 1971. It was a handsome collection that she had wanted to call *A Gwendolyn Brooks Omnibus*. It included *A Street in Bronzeville*, *Annie Allen*, *Maud Martha*, *The Bean Eaters*, and *In the Mecca*. Harper & Row, for whatever reason, had wanted to exclude *In the Mecca*, but Gwendolyn wisely had prevailed. She wanted to present a whole picture of her work up until that time. As far as the collection's title, Gwendolyn had settled for *The World of Gwendolyn Brooks*. That, too, was a wise decision. The volume welcomed readers to a whole way of life as perceived by a quiet genius.

At the same time, she moved deeper into her work with Broadside Press. With the publication of *Riot*, she had written a note to Broadside Press: "Dudley Randall has been *given Riot* (for the duration of *his* life)."[8] This indicated that she was turning back her royalties to the press and would in no way profit from the publication of *Riot*. Yet she was a stickler for a clear accounting of her royalties. She was generous, not foolish.

Aloneness was a slight volume, published with Broadside, also in 1971. It was targeted as a children's book, but the poem had been conceived as a poem for anyone. With its sweet sketches, it explored the difference between aloneness and loneliness. Loneliness was a feeling of lack, and aloneness, of course, a benefit. But most beneficial was love. That is a lesson that Gwendolyn taught to children, women, and men—to find the strength and pleasure in being alone, but to recognize the joys, strength, and comfort of love. All of her life, Gwendolyn had dwelled in the embrace of aloneness as she sat on her back steps studying the sky or sat at her desk composing poems and stories, making aloneness a creative space. And as a loving person she had welcomed the presence of love, giving it and receiving it. Yet she had felt the sting of loneliness when she had been rejected because of her color or lack of certain social attributes. She knew that love trumped loneliness and sometimes aloneness. This is a message that would resonate not only with children but also with the many black women of marriage age who found themselves single. In its way, the poem offers a feminist message. As women we are sufficient unto ourselves and the joys that life provides.

In February 1971, *Jump Bad*, the anthology of the Gwendolyn Brooks Writers Workshop, which met in her home, was published by Broadside. It is significant that *Jump Bad* is described as a "New Chicago Anthology presented by Gwendolyn Brooks." She chose to say "presented" as opposed to "edited" to give power to the poets and writers in the collection. She had abridged them in no way. They were as they were. She simply gave them her seal of approval. It was sufficient. The anthology was dedicated to Hoyt W. Fuller, "Great Editor—Warm Educator." He was, with Gwendolyn, a godparent of a generation of poets and writers.

The anthology was named by the gifted poet and writer Carolyn Rodgers after an action that black folks described as "jumping bad"— an aggressive, pugilistic stance. If one jumped bad, he or she was ready to fight and acted like it. Gwendolyn admired that fighting spirit of this new breed of poets and writers. They were Jump Badders: Rodgers, Don Lee, Walter Bradford, Sigemonde Wimberli, Ronda Davis, Johari Amini, Mike Cook, James Cunningham, Sharon Scott, Peggy Kenner, Carl Clark, and Liyatta (formerly Doris Turner). These poets and writers did things their way, following no rules learned in creative-writing classes. They were free and fearless. They succeeded and they failed on their own terms, and that is what Gwendolyn supported. They wrote organically out of their own experiences, as Fuller would say. Gwendolyn endorsed this bold exploration. She still believed in craft, however, and looked favorably on the work of Lee as an innovator and craftsman.

Jump Bad was evidence of those lively meetings at Gwendolyn's home. It was also a testament to the hours of talk and debate about matters of consequence—revolution, rejection of white values and awards and credentials, life-maps for each, and the development of black style, craft, and criticism.

Gwendolyn did more than present the works of Jump Badders in 1971, however. She also edited a collection of the best Broadside Press works of the first five years of the publishing house. As she edited *A Broadside Treasury*, Gwendolyn was of firm mind. She was not swayed in her selections by personal regard or fear of repercussion. Dudley Randall chaffed at her selections and was startled at her independence of choice. In correspondence from February 9, 1971, Randall noted that he had had the chance to watch Gwendolyn work on the treasury while he was in town for a book party for the book *To Gwen with Love*. "Gwen putting the book together with digital skill. Gwen the tough editor defending her choices—24 poems by Nikki [Giovanni] and only 9 by Randall (is she losing her mind!) Is Nikki 3 times better than me?"[9] Gwendolyn let nothing stand in the way between her discerning eye and the poem.

BAM, the Black Arts Movement, was bustling with energy, activities, and personalities from the mid-1960s through the mid-1970s. The South Side Community Art Center kept its doors open, and it was an early home for the OBAC Writers Workshop. By 1969, the workshop had moved to the home it would maintain for a number of years at 77 East Thirty-Fifth Street until *Black World* magazine was discontinued and Hoyt W. Fuller would leave the city for Atlanta in the spring of 1976. The workshop, with its connection to Gwendolyn, was just part of the vibrancy and vitality of the period. All manner of people would come through the doors of OBAC: bus drivers; students from the many schools and universities in Chicago, including Loyola, Northwestern, the University of Chicago, the University of Illinois; professors from the University of Chicago (George E. Kent) and University of Illinois (Philip Royster); unemployed people; and schoolteachers.

OBAC writers and poets were a part of the literary flowering that included black publishing houses like Free Black Press of Useni

Eugene Perkins and Third World Press, founded by Don Lee, with Carolyn Rodgers and Johari Amini coming aboard. There were also dance troupes, drummer groups, jazz groups, and theater groups such as ETA Theater, Kuumba Theater, and Black Ensemble Theater.

Poets and writers came from out of town: Dennis Brutus exiled from South Africa, Ruwa Chiri from Zimbabwe, and Keorapetse Kgositsile from South Africa, who would become the poet laureate of South Africa, all from the Motherland. Out-of-towners visited Chicago often as well, including the esteemed poet and writer Mari Evans from Indianapolis; Eugene Redmond, poet and critic from East St. Louis, Illinois; Amiri Baraka, deemed the father of the Black Arts Movement, to speak to overflow crowds.

All of these people were friends of Gwendolyn or known to her. Especially close was Val Gray Ward, founder of Kuumba Theater, whom Gwendolyn described or mentioned in more than one poem. When Gwendolyn wrote about Ward, it was with affection and warmth. Ward was a longtime friend with whom Gwendolyn spent many afternoons over lunch at black restaurants or at the Walnut Room in Marshall Field's department store downtown. Ward noted that when Gwendolyn was with the new breed of black poets, she "was like a young girl," vivacious and energized. Ward, from all-black Mound Bayou, Mississippi, and Gwendolyn, from Bronzeville, related to each other as women of core-black culture. They were daughters of the Root, committed to the arts and to the black liberation struggle.

The Afro-Arts Theater was known for its cultural education of children and its language lessons of Kiswahili, Arabic, and Yoruba, and for its exuberant programs of music, dance and poetry. Its in-house musicians were not so much interested in entertainment, a momentary escapism from the stresses of everyday life, but "inner-attainment," the spiritual enlightenment, delight and clarity of black people. They were there to raise consciousness and keep it raised. A group of young black musicians called the Jazzmen had merged with Cohran's Artistic Heritage Ensemble to become the Pharaohs, a thirteen-piece band who played at the Afro-Arts Theater. Later Maurice White and others of the Pharaohs became the spectacular and phenomenally successful group Earth, Wind and Fire.

Val Gray Ward was behind the program at Chicago's Afro-Arts Theater, formerly the Oakland Theater, honoring Gwendolyn as a "great writer and beloved black woman." Proceeds for the event, held in December of 1969, went to the DuSable Museum of African American History; to the Black Women's Committee for the Care and Protection of Our Children, with its Gwendolyn Brooks library room; and to the Afro-Arts Theater itself.

Gwendolyn described the gathering as "the most stirring tribute of my life, the most significant."[10] Included in that memorable program in the spacious but intimate theater were performances or readings by Val Gray Ward and the Kuumba Players, Phil Cohran and the Artistic Heritage Ensemble, the Pharaohs, the Malcolm X Community College Chorus, Carolyn Rodgers, Sister Zubena (Cynthia Conley), Dudley Randall, Lerone Bennett, Margaret Burroughs, Margaret Danner Cunningham, Johari Amini, Don L. Lee, Walter Bradford, Useni Eugene Perkins, Ronda Davis, Sonia Sanchez, Sigemonde Wimberli, painters Jeff Donaldson, Jon Lockard, and Edward Christmas who had painted Gwendolyn on the Wall of Respect, jewelry designer Norbert Wilkinson (Sika Dwimfo). "And—the Blackstone Rangers came, in force!—with tokens of affection, earnest personal Congratulations."[11] The dancers danced African joy! What a day it was!

Gwendolyn had received many honorary doctorates by this point, been honored with much fanfare, but nothing approached that day at the Afro-Arts Theater. The day itself was poetry, a heightened reality.

Whereas the exultation at the Afro-Arts Theater in December 1969 had been a community affair, Gwendolyn was also warmly endorsed by the Talented Tenth in a more formal setting in September 1971, when she was honored along with dancer Katherine Dunham and Duke Ellington at the second annual awards banquet of the Black Academy of Arts and Letters, at New York's Waldorf Astoria hotel. Dunham was honored for Outstanding Achievement in the Arts, the Medal of Merit was given to Ellington, and Gwendolyn was honored for Outstanding Achievement in Letters. The honor was appreciated by Gwendolyn, for the members of the academy included people she held in high esteem, such as Lerone Bennett, Ossie Davis, Ruby Dee, and John Oliver Killens.

The anthology *To Gwen with Love* was the result of the celebration at the Afro-Arts Theater at the end of 1969. Published in 1971, it was the ultimate valentine for the poet and included praise poems and testimony from fifty poets and writers, young and old, known and unknown. Edited by Patricia L. Brown, Don Lee, and Francis Ward, the volume was published by Johnson Publishing Company. The outstanding cover art by Jeff Donaldson was a painting of the poet seated on an African stool to signify royalty. The titles of her books, written in watercolors, cascaded around her. In the painting, Gwendolyn smiled wryly and gazed into the distance. She wore a crown-like Afro and, around that, a halo. The painting was inspired, conveying Gwendolyn as a cultural Queen Mother. The loving praises enclosed in the book would only be bestowed upon one beloved for who she is both inside and outside by all in her realm. Truly, the dark, quiet girl, once rejected, had entered a new black moment in history in which she was regarded as royalty.

Gwendolyn was surprised to have been so honored and loved by the Black Arts/Black Consciousness movements. She was their queen, and she ruled with commitment, generosity, kindness, and an exquisite pen.

CHAPTER EIGHT

Journeys

Gwendolyn Brooks was riding the current of Black Consciousness with her Black Community, her Black Family at large. At the same time, the anti-apartheid movement in South Africa was rising to prominence, the women's movement had gathered voice and volume, and the movement against the Vietnam War was at its peak. These world-transforming movements would impact Gwendolyn and enlarge her vision. She journeyed forth, firm in her racial and cultural identity, always recognizing that this was the source of her deep humanity and artistry.

Since the writers' conference at Fisk University in 1967, Gwendolyn had undergone a profound shift, and the shift pulled at her marriage with Henry. As she aligned herself with the ideas of the new-breed poets, Henry objected. Nora heard her mother say to her father, "You middle-aged people make me so mad!" Old issues that had lain dormant in the marriage rose to the surface, and the couple grew apart. Matters were exacerbated in 1968 in an argument over Nora's missed curfew, and Gwendolyn was driven to tears. Nora had never seen her mother cry before. Within a year, Gwendolyn and Henry had separated.

About that separation, Gwendolyn was vague, suggesting simply that the marriage had run its course.[1] In fact, she had suffered the personal pain of disconnection from her life mate. She no longer had to prepare three meals a day for a husband and children. The husband had packed up and gone; the children were grown. She no longer had to iron a fresh shirt for Henry each day. With this new freedom from housewifery and even motherhood, Gwendolyn was able to travel more extensively and work even more productively during this time, publishing her own books, *Riot*, the children's book *Aloneness*, and *Family Pictures*, and working on the collections *A Broadside Treasury* and *Jump Bad*. In addition, she edited essays in her magazine, *The Black Position*, published by Broadside Press.

In 1971, she traveled on assignment for *Ebony* magazine to Montgomery, Alabama, and wrote a piece that she described as "verse journalism," a genre of her own invention. In verse journalism, she merged two interests from her childhood: poetry and journalism. That same year, she accepted a commission to write a poem, "Black Steel: Joe Frazier and Muhammad Ali," which was published in the program for the "Fight of the Century," held March 8, 1971, in Madison Square Garden. One would not have expected Gwendolyn to pen a poem on boxing, but the point of her selection was that she represented another kind of black excellence. She was a female champion.

In 1969, *The Black Woman*, Toni Cade Bambara's groundbreaking feminist anthology, was published, opening a new discussion on gender equality, race, class, and social justice inside the black community and giving voice to black women on these crucial issues. *Ms.* began publishing in July 1972. Its notable black contributor was Alice Walker. *Essence* magazine, for black women, began publishing in May 1970. It was known to tackle weighty subjects, as well as trends in fashion, travel, and hair styles. Gwendolyn was interviewed by the magazine's editor, Ida Lewis, in the spring of 1971.

In the interview, Gwendolyn talked about the end of her marriage. She remarked on the pleasures of being a single, independent woman and made it clear that marriage was no longer a situation she desired. "I can say that I have no intention of ever getting married again," Gwendolyn said. "No, not to God. One general reason for this decision is that marriage is a hard, demanding state. Especially if you're a woman, you have to set aside yourself constantly. Although I did it during my marriage, I couldn't again. After having a year of solitude, I realize that this is what is right for me, to be able to control my life."[2]

Gwendolyn did acknowledge that Henry had been an affirming husband for her as a writer. "He encouraged me in my writing all along," she said. "He was very pleased when any good thing happened to me, although I know that, being a man, he did have problems adjusting to what I was doing. Often we discussed his own literary ambitions. He hasn't really put them to test yet." It must be difficult to have two lights turned all the way up at once in the same room. One only needs one. Or could two bright lights only bring a great glow?

At this time, panels were often held on the role of the black woman in "the revolution" or on black male-female relationships. Tension between the sexes was of paramount concern. This was heightened or clarified by the women's liberation movement. Feminism and Black Consciousness often argued with each other, and Gwendolyn spoke to and for each.

> Relations between men and women seem disordered to me. I was asked recently how I felt about Women's Lib. I think Women's Lib is not for black women for the time being, because black men need their women beside them, supporting them in these very tempestuous days. I made this comment in [the historian] Horace Bond's class as well, and a young man asked me, "What do you mean, 'for the time being?' I said, "Well, that will depend on how you men treat us. As our struggle goes on, if you treat us considerately we may never subscribe to 'the movement.'" . . . I did say that it's entirely wrong, of course, for women to be denied the same job income men have. When it comes to that, black women should be fighting for equal pay just as white women.[3]

After several years apart, Gwendolyn and Henry reunited. The reunion was casual enough. She had called him to invite him to a family function, as he was much beloved by her mother and late father. Henry, in turn, had loved both her mother and father. When Gwendolyn called, Henry, anxious for her refined ear, had asked to share his new poetry with her. So they resumed as they had begun—with the love of poetry connecting them.

Gwendolyn had long said that on the level of pure companionship, she and Henry got along fine. There is an old West African saying, "Talking together is loving one another." When Gwendolyn and Henry came together again, they could talk in a way that did not need explanation. They swam in the same pool of memory: the apartment on Sixty-Third Street, the Visionaries, the parties, the births of Hank and Nora. There was a shorthand between them. They began to date as they had when they were young. Poetry wove its spell between them.

Gwendolyn had enjoyed her years of independence, and she never could conceive of marrying again. But the comforts of a tried-and-true love relationship lured her back to Henry. They had so much to share. She had enjoyed the benefits of aloneness, but love in addition to this valued aloneness was pleasing. She and Henry gave each other space.

On November 5, 1973, there appeared an item in the "Charlie Cherokee" gossip column of the *Chicago Defender*: "Poet Gwendolyn Brooks and her husband have reunited. To celebrate the occasion, they had a second honeymoon in London. So Splitsville is forgotten."

In January 1974, Raymond Brooks, Gwendolyn's brother, died of natural causes. He was fifty-five. He left four children, Ray Jr., Paulette, David, and Dorothea. Gwendolyn and her mother, Keziah, shared their grief.

Perhaps the loss of her brother compelled Gwendolyn to enjoy life on its own terms, to take even more time for herself and to share certain things with Henry. She had long dreamed of going to Ghana, in West Africa. So in the summer of 1974, Gwendolyn and Henry journeyed there together. They experienced the large cities of Accra and Kumasi, and they were overwhelmed at the Cape Coast, where they visited Elmina Castle, the location of despair from which Africans were shipped into slavery in the West or murdered before they left the shores of the Gold Coast.

Gwendolyn and Henry settled in at the Ambassador Hotel and set out to see the city. As most tourists are easily identified by locals, they were approached by a young man named Bayour Ameru, who offered to act as their driver and guide. Ameru seemed to be known by everyone, as people called out to him as they rode around. He appeared to be well-regarded.

After Henry and Gwendolyn made the usual tourist stop at a department store, where Gwendolyn purchased dresses, scarves, and other finery, she made more unusual purchases of candy and popcorn. Then she and Henry did something most significant. They went to a school where Gwendolyn gave the popcorn and candy to the school children. She relished their smiles and enjoyed their joy. This says so much about her core identity and her commitment to children everywhere. She was not complete unless she was enriching the lives of children in some way.

The couple concluded their journey with a trip to Kumasi, where they visited friends of Gwendolyn's publisher, the poet Dudley Randall. The husband, Leroy Mitchell, was teaching art at the University of Kumasi. He was a painter. His wife, Dorothy, instructed Gwendolyn on the changing status of women in Ghana. Just as American women had changed, so had Ghanaian women. They were no longer as submissive but were businesswomen: market women selling their produce in their stalls in the open-air markets.

With the Mitchells, Gwendolyn and Henry toured the modern grounds of the University of Kumasi and the rest of the city. Freight trucks called "mammy wagons" carried passengers and goods to and fro, and whizzed by with witty phrases emblazoned on the side, like "Friends Today—Enemies Tomorrow."

They went to Accra, cacao capital of the world, from which Ghana derived much of its wealth. They relished the ancient arts and crafts of Ghana, the cloth and carvings, but Accra was also a modern city. Their visit was a study in contrasts.

One day, Gwendolyn and Henry encountered a man burdened by a life of miseries. Gwendolyn, ever the kind-hearted one, gave the man some money. Henry told her she had "been taken." Gwendolyn no doubt was used to being generous to beggars. That was the way her parents responded to those in need.

The heart of the two sojourners' journey to Ghana was not to the big cities of Accra or Kumasi but a trip that was a two-and-a-half-hour, comfortable bus ride to the Cape Coast. Once there, they took a taxi to the place that so many black Americans sought out when they came to Ghana—Elmina Castle.

Elmina Castle and Goree Island off the coast of Senegal are the two heart-wrenching sites from which kidnapped Africans were shipped out to Europe, the Americas, and the West Indies. Most black Americans who visit Elmina Castle describe a soul-shaking epiphany that devolves into a nightmare memory. Gwendolyn and Henry were no exceptions.

She wrote about the details of the castle—the dank floor, "the ancient, cruel walls." She described the small dungeons in which the most resistant Africans were murdered or deprived of food, water, and fresh air. And if that did not kill them, their throats were slit methodically.[4]

The tour guide told them how the most comely African girls and women were taken from the prison to the governor's quarters, where they were raped until they were impregnated. Once pregnant, they were freed. "And the mulattoes you see in the town now," the guide informed them, "are the descendants of such white and Black unions." Gwendolyn wrote about this matter-of-factly.

Then the part of the Elmina experience that led to the African American experience began. Gwendolyn and Henry were seized by the horror of it. I know of an African American scholar who lost the use of her limbs at this point in the remembrance. Gwendolyn and Henry, too, were overwhelmed by the spirits of the stolen and lost sons and daughters of villages and cities as they walked down a hall deep in Elmina Castle. Bats roosted overhead.

Henry and Gwendolyn saw where the governor looked in upon the enslaved Africans. They ventured further into the cells where black people died or waited to be shipped to new shores. Gwendolyn felt what all black people feel, "exhaustion, ache, rage, and a drained and helpless oh." The walls of Elmina "shrieked"; "calling walls." This was a spiritual experience, psychologically wrenching.[5]

After the cruelty of Elmina, Gwendolyn and Henry lunched and sat among the Ghanaians, watching the people and the lively land. Gwendolyn befriended a girl, one of two engaged in braiding hair. Surely the little girl who sold fruit pies would grow up to be a market woman.

In Kumasi, Gwendolyn and Henry were told the story of events that led to a great war between the British and the Ashanti people. The British colonizer wanted to take a seat upon the royal Ashanti stool in which was invested the traditional power of the people. The Ashanti people resisted and waged war. This was the War of the Golden Stool in 1900.

Ghanaians have a sure sense of their African identity. Henry noted this and brought it up to a Ghanaian. He said, "We Blacks in the United States envy you. YOU ARE AFRIKANS. You know this country is YOURS.—that you BELONG here. We Blacks in the United States don't know what we are." She had looked at him with impatient semi-contempt. "YOU AMERICAINE!"[6]

Gwendolyn seemed troubled by the Ghanaian response to Henry's point of view. Identity was not so simple a subject to African Americans, who are American by birth but not by rights rendered and treatment. Blacks in America had never been made to feel American; we are American in spite of the country itself.

In April 1975, the *Chicago Defender* ran a caricature of a curly-coiffed, smiling Gwendolyn standing between two books with her name on them. She was leaning her shoulder and arm on *Annie Allen* and braced her opposite hip against *The Wall*. She had skinny legs and wore big white pumps as in the fashion of a cartoon character. The caption underneath the caricature read: "Gwendolyn Brooks, poet laureate of Illinois and world famous, will be featured subject in the weekend Accent."

The caricature conveys Gwendolyn in a dilemma, leaning on her achievement as a Pulitzer Prize winner for the obscure *Annie Allen* and bracing herself with *The Wall*, which technically is not a book but a poem representing her welcoming into the ranks of the Black Arts Movement, a more community-oriented art. In addition, the caricature suggests something conflicted in Gwendolyn herself. Perhaps her identity issues had not been fully resolved. To portray her with curly hair as opposed to her Afro is to suggest that she had not completely reinvented herself. Or she leaned on *Annie Allen* to be who she was. She was more like *Annie Allen*, upon which she draped her torso, than *The Wall*. She was not as black conscious as she said she was, the drawing conveys.

According to Gwendolyn's daughter, Nora, perhaps this "cute cartoon is a case of where somebody has put their own personal issues on somebody else. They didn't realize what she was saying before 1967 and didn't fully appreciate who she had been before 1967 in her work. It was a matter of style change. She had not dumbed down her work, but stripped it to a leaner style."

Nora has a unique understanding of her mother's work and has even been an inspiration for it. "*The Tiger Who Wore White Gloves* is me. I was about eight or ten. It was Halloween. I was all excited about going out for Halloween. I went out in a tiger costume. I went out and came back in and got my little white church gloves. Mama, when she stopped laughing, said, 'I'm going to write a poem about this.'

"When Mama wrote a poem about it, the tiger was a he. When I was in my thirties, a woman asked her, 'Why is the tiger a he?' Mama and I said, 'Hmmm.' It had never occurred to her that the tiger should be a she."

Perhaps when it was time to write the poem, other cultural and literary references came to bear, and a male tiger made better sense. *The Tiger Who Wore White Gloves* was a charming children's book published in 1975 by Third World Press. The title tells the story and the message. A tiger does not wear white gloves. If a tiger wears white gloves, he or she is not being a tiger. A tiger should just be a tiger. That is enough. Gwendolyn taught children a message of self-acceptance and celebration. What you are you are. There is a clarity of identity in this. By extension, black people should not try to be other than black. To do so is absurd.

In a literary context, Gwendolyn was giving a sly if unconscious response to William Blake's classic poem.

THE TYGER
Tyger Tyger, burning bright,
In the forests of the night'
What immortal hand or eye,
Could frame thy fearful symmetry?

In what distant deeps or skies.
Burnt the fire of thine eyes?
On what wings dare he aspire?
What the hand, dare seize the fire?

In what shoulder, & what art,
Could twist the sinews of thy heart?
And when thy heart began to beat,
What dread hand? & what dread feet?[7]

Blake's poem was written in 1794. I am sure Gwendolyn was more than familiar with it. The fierce creature who is conjured here would never wear white gloves. This gives us a stronger sense of her perspective. There is an innate and experiential power in the tiger that must not be tamed by inappropriate convention. *The Tiger Who Wore White Gloves* is a children's story, but its message is deeper than children can yet fully conceive.

In the poems "The Life of Lincoln West" and "The Tiger Who Wore White Gloves," the ideas of self-acceptance, self-affirmation, and healthy self-love were a leitmotif countering the pervasive presence of racism and colorism, and building self-esteem and healthy egos in black children. In actuality, this leitmotif of healthy self-love runs subtly through her entire oeuvre.

Gwendolyn turned down a well-paying, secure career in teaching in order to pursue the full-time life of the writer, as Langston Hughes had done. Amid her travel and readings and writing, she enjoyed fellowship in her black community. She participated in Chicago's African Liberation Day celebrations and was one of many esteemed writers, including Shirley Graham DuBois, Sonia Sanchez, Mari Evans, Haki Madhubuti (formerly Don Lee), Hoyt W. Fuller, and Sam "The Spook Who Sat by the Door" Greenlee, who also attended OBAC's eight-and-a-half-year celebration.

All the while Gwendolyn wrote, and in writing taught others to write. In *A Capsule Course in Black Poetry Writing* (1975, coauthored with Keorapetse Kgositsile, Haki Madhubuti, and Dudley Randall), she advised: "Try telling the reader a little less. He'll, she'll love you more, if you allow him to do a little digging. Not too much, but some." In *Young Poet's Primer* (1980), she cautioned "Your poem does not need to tell your reader everything. A little mystery is fascinating. Too much is irritating." In the *Chicago Defender*, May 8, 1965, she described a poet as "one who crystallizes vagueness, filters experience until it can be held familiarly in the hand." She does this in her "new" way in the poem "Aurora," written for the inauguration of the Illinois governor. The language is deliciously alliterative and dazzling, but its meanings less hidden. It is open, public art for a public function. It sets a high standard for the genre.

Whereas "Aurora" was a high point in Gwendolyn's quest for poetry that spoke to the people of the state of Illinois at least, the poems of *Beckonings* did not measure up to her expectations for new work that would captivate the masses of black people who were not lovers of traditional poetry. *Beckonings* (1975) was Gwendolyn's least favorite volume, and she found the twelve-poem collection to be her least successful, even though she was attempting to move in another direction in her art. Still, one of her favorite poems to read to audiences was from this collection, her tribute to the good sense and contentment of domestic animals.

HORSES GRAZE

Cows graze.
Horses graze.
They
eat
eat
eat.
Their graceful heads
are bowed
bowed
bowed
in majestic oblivion.
They are nobly oblivious
to your follies,
your inflation,
the knocks and nettles of administration.
They
eat
eat
eat.
And at the crest of their brute satisfaction,
with wonderful gentleness, in affirmation,
they lift their clean calm eyes and they lie down
and love the world.
They speak with their companions.
They do not wish that they were otherwhere.
Perhaps they know that creature feet may press
only a few earth inches at a time,
that earth is anywhere earth,
that an eye may see,

wherever it may be, the
Immediate arc, alone, of life, of love.
In Sweden,
China,
Africa,
in India or Maine,
the animals are sane; they
know and know and know
there's ground below
and sky
up high.

In "Horses Graze," style and content are married. Gwendolyn addressed, with a gentle ease, the sanity of animals and their reverent sense of themselves on the planet.

She appeared to enjoy reading this poem, as if she were imparting the message of her own satisfaction in her position as one of God's creatures who is contentedly aware of where she stands between earth and sky. Gwendolyn's feet were firmly planted on the ground even as she studied the sky as she had done when she was a little girl.

The year 1976 was one of achievement. She received the prestigious Shelley Memorial Award from the Poetry Society of America and was the first black woman elected to the National Institute of Arts and Letters. That same year, a play based on her work, *Among All This You Stand Like a Fine Brown Stone*, written and directed by Vantile Whitfield, was produced in Washington, DC. It later was produced at Val Gray Ward's Kuumba Theater and the ETA Theater, both in Chicago.

There is no passing quite like the death of the mother. The vessel out of which one was poured is broken. One looks back in emptiness and longing, and it is overwhelming. This was especially the case with Gwendolyn and her mother, Keziah. Keziah had not only birthed her but she had propelled her into the world as a poet. She had given her space and a sense of specialness. Keziah had what Gwendolyn called "nerve." She had nerve enough to believe that her daughter could be a poet and took her to meet esteemed poets to give her direction. Keziah had been her firm foundation, her root, and her rock. So Gwendolyn had to let go of her rock and stand sturdily as a woman without the benefit of being a beloved daughter. She found another rock in her daughter, Nora.

Keziah's decline began recognizably when her purse was snatched as she came home from a shopping trip. Two boys who knew her chased the thieves and retrieved her purse. But the damage had been done. She lost her sense of security and began to decline like her neighborhood.

Gwendolyn's mother was replenished by the publication of her book of autobiographical essays and meditations when she was eighty-eight, *The Voice and Other Short Stories*. Gwendolyn held a book party for Keziah one sunny weekend day in the crowded gallery of the South Side Community Art Center.

Then her mother began to experience forgetfulness. One Sunday Gwendolyn came to pick her up for her regular, richly anticipated Sunday service, and Keziah had no idea why her daughter had come for her. She never went to church again.

In the spring of 1977, Gwendolyn and Henry took Keziah to a lovely brunch. Keziah exclaimed over the restaurant, the food she ate with such pleasure, and Gwendolyn's "kindness." Because Gwendolyn had to catch a plane so that she could go to do a reading, Henry did not perform his usual ritual of walking Keziah to her door and into the house. He left her at the door. Once Gwendolyn reached her campus destination, her booking agent, Beryl Zitch, called to tell her the distressing news. Keziah's home had been burglarized while they had been at brunch. The thieves had taken what was easy to carry and sell—radio, television, fans, phonograph, and valuables. Henry had come over and sealed and bolted Keziah's door, but the spirit of trespass was profound. Her psychological boundaries had been invaded. Even though the thieves were later caught, Keziah was never the same. She lost interest in food.

There began the long conversation about what was best for her mother in terms of housing and security. Keziah felt most comfortable in her own home. At a time when her furnace was not working and Henry was working to install a new one, Keziah had come to stay with the Blakelys. Keziah was very uncomfortable while she was not in her own home. Gwendolyn and other family members had to arrange to visit her often to check in on her when she was home alone.

As Keziah's health worsened, she stopped eating and stopped taking her medicine. She had to be hospitalized at Michael Reese Hospital. Eventually, she was brought back home under a doctor and nurse's care.

Keziah was happy to be at home, and Gwendolyn was happy that her mother was home as well. "I am peaceful," Keziah said. "Thank you." When Gwendolyn bathed her, her normally willful mother was compliant—too compliant. She refused to eat. But she was more responsive to her nurse, as is the case with many older patients. Finally, on Tuesday, March 14, 1978, at 8 p.m., when Gwendolyn was coming back home after giving a reading at the University of Vermont, Keziah Wims Brooks released her spirit. Born March 1, 1888, she was ninety years old at the time of her passing. Her daughter had given her a birthday party two weeks before.

It was Nora who told her mother as Gwendolyn rode back on the train. In a time of no cell phones, the train had pulled into a tiny stop and Gwendolyn had called home and learned of her mother's death. She took a plane the rest of the way. From the moment that Nora told Gwendolyn of her mother's passing, Nora was her mother's ready comfort, always available to answer her grief. As Gwendolyn had been to her dying mother, Nora was to her grieving one.

After Keziah's passing, Gwendolyn found a note marked "To Gwendolyn" written and saved in her mother's old desk. "Dear Daughter, I am truly appreciative of your many kind deeds. They have given me much comfort and happiness. I hope that your success continues and that you will be happy throughout life. Love, Mama."[8] This note meant a great deal to Gwendolyn, as in life her mother had never been demonstrative. Gwendolyn had always longed for her mother to say, "I love you." Now those cherished words came.

In 1982, relations between the United States and the USSR were still cold. When Gwendolyn traveled there with a group of fellow American writers that summer, it was an international undertaking of some import.

Gwendolyn explored the country with Studs Terkel, the oral historian of Division Street, America, and Chicago radio personality, and his wife, Ida. Also traveling were Erica Jong, critically respected and best-selling feminist author of *Fear of Flying*; Irving Stone, known for his biographical novels, notably *The Agony and the Ecstasy*, on Michelangelo, and *Lust for Life*, on van Gogh; Arthur Schlesinger Jr., Pulitzer Prize–winning author of *A Thousand Days*, about John F. Kennedy's White House years; Robert Bly, poet and National Book Award winner for *The Light Around the Body*; and author Susan Sontag, known at the time for her essay collection *On Photography*.[9]

The group went at the invitation of Harrison Salisbury to attend the Sixth Annual Soviet-American Writers Conference. Salisbury was the former assistant managing editor and associate editor of the *New York Times*, an expert on Russia, and the author of *The 900 Days: The Siege of Leningrad*. The American writers would spend several days in Kiev meeting with Soviet writers and then several more days in Leningrad and Moscow.

In Moscow, they met their tour guide, Mikhail Kusmenko, a twenty-one-year-old who spoke excellent English. The personable, young Mikhail, affectionately called Misha, guided them through Kiev, where they stayed at the Kiev Hotel.

In a great room of the hotel, the Soviet and American writers assembled at separate tables. On the second day, progressive, affable, humane Studs Terkel suggested that the writers should "mix it up." After much moving around, Terkel wound up seated with the Soviets and everyone else remained seated at their tables.

Another standout who attempted to foster change was Erica Jong, who kept asking of the Soviets, "Where are the women writers? Where are the woman writers?" She was told that they were "all on vacation. Out in the country." (In a nation as repressive as the Soviet Union, that could have meant anything.) Gwendolyn noted that the male Soviet writers were familiar with the beautiful Jong's sexy books. They assumed she would be superficial, but her speech proved her brilliance, and she was as described by Gwendolyn, "brilliant, informed, managed, sane."

After Robert Bly read his poetry while playing his mandolin, and the Soviet writer Nikolai Fedorenko cautioned him against roaming while reading and losing his simultaneous translator, Gwendolyn read "The Life of Lincoln West."

Of course, "The Life of Lincoln West" is a rather sad narrative poem with a light touch to make it less painful. In the end, the little black boy who was deemed ugly found a sense of self-worth because he was described by two white strangers as not only "ugly and odd," usual assessments for him, but also "the real thing." "The real thing" lingers. Fedorenko, the Soviet writer, loved the story because he had missed its point. He responded with a story of his own "about a dear little Black boy who had wandered into the midst of heretofore dense folk (including himself). This little boy everyone found *touchable* and absolutely *darling* with his nice white teeth and nice rough hair. Everyone *loved* to pat his nice rough hair."

Gwendolyn was appalled by this response, and even more appalled that the white writers, American and Soviet, were "pleased with" her. Her rage simmered and grew until two sessions later she asked Harrison Salisbury to give her the floor. She read this clarifying statement:

I agree with Mr. Aitmatov—a nuclear blast would abolish everything, including all aspects of ethnic concern for ethnic bliss. Nevertheless, I am going to call attention to *Blackness*, a matter no one else here feels any reason to cite. No one *else* here feels any reason to cite Blackness because on the Soviet side there is very little association with Blacks. Soviets see very few. And on the American side there is as little association with Blacks as can comfortably be managed, although there is great opportunity in the United States of America, where there are many many many many many MANY Blacks. Well, all of you must understand that the planet is swarming with *dark* people. The other day Nikolai Federenko, droll, dry, and when he's right AND when he's wrong, a strangely fascinating personality, out of the kindness of his heart (and I received it as such) "comforted me" with a tale of a *dear* little Black boy whom everyone found *touchable* and absolutely darling with his nice white teeth . . . Then Mr. Federenko said something very large: WE NEVER PAID ATTENTION AT ALL TO THE FACT THAT HE WAS NEGRO!!!!!!! WELL, I *have* to reply to this. Essential Blacks—by that I mean Blacks who are not trying desperately to be white—are happy to have you notice that they do not look like you. *Essential* Blacks don't want to look like you. You're OK, they're OK. We essential Blacks do *not* think it would be a blessing if everyone was of the same hue. Personally, I like the idea of a garden rich with varieties of flowers. Although I like roses, I like other flowers too. So please DO, Mr. Nikolai Federenko, go right ahead and *notice* that Blacks really look and *are* quite different from yourself. Go right ahead and PAY ATTENTION TO THAT FACT.[10]

In all the time that she was in the Soviet Union, Gwendolyn saw very few black people. She saw a few black men, a team of basketball players, students, and the like, but no black women other than her own reflection in the looking glass.

The American writers visited Kiev and Leningrad and saw the sites of German annihilation and the beautiful museum filled with van Goghs and jewels. Amid the ornate history came a bit of histrionics from Gwendolyn's fellow American traveler, Susan Sontag, the striking Jewish intellectual darling. Gwendolyn was being interviewed for an article titled "What It Means to Be Black" by an editor of a Russian magazine, *Foreign Literature*. Sontag interrupted and began to give her answer. Gwendolyn interrupted the interrupter, "Why do you turn from me to her with this question? Obviously, being Black,

I know more about what it means to be black than does *she*." Sontag was not happy. According to Gwendolyn, she was enraged. "How dare you assume such nonsense," Sontag said. They were entering a palace, removing their shoes to protect the floors. Seated on the bench together, Sontag was "screaming. My outrageous fancy that I know more about being black than *she* knows has pushed her to wild-eyed frenzy." Sontag continued to scream. "Finally, she utters an unforgettable sentence—which I can report exactly because I wrote it down immediately: 'I TURN MY BACK UPON YOU.' She carried off this awesome threat. She turns her back upon me, with a gr-r-eat shake of her bottom to appall me. I am ass—uredly impressed."[11]

One gathers here a sense of Gwendolyn's great sense of humor. Her response to Sontag's sense of superiority and rage at her loss of white privilege to speak on behalf of black people is endearing. Gwendolyn was welcomed with the other Americans at the Leningrad Writers Union. She was especially well received when she read a poem to Misha, their friendly young tour guide. She learned that the Soviets took poetry quite seriously. In America, a poet is doing well when his or her book sells a few thousand copies. In the USSR, poetry sold by the tens of thousands.

On the way back to America, stopping in Copenhagen, the group could feel the change in social climate. Gwendolyn felt "hope." In Russia, she had felt "sanction." In America, she was happy to see black people, waves of black people, and black women like herself stepping out of mirrors and striding around.

In her sojourns, Gwendolyn had also moved forward with her words, traveling light. She did not pack them tightly. She carried as much meaning as she could in fewer words. She addressed black people. Her people were her concern, although she would stop to write a kind poem to the young man who had been her tour guide in Russia. Her humanity brimmed in her words.

In *Primer for Blacks* (1980, Third World Press), she sent out a call to all black people. In doing so she annihilated colorism and any divisions and issues among black people based on the unhealthy obsession with skin color.

> *Blackness*
> *stretches over the land.*
> *Blackness—*
> *the Blackness of it,*
> *the rust-red of it,*
> *the milk and cream of it,*
> *the tan and yellow-tan of it,*
> *the deep-brown middle brown high brown of it,*
> *the "olive" and ochre of it—*
> *Blackness*
> *marches on.*

With this poetic gesture, Gwendolyn would heal her black family at large of any self-inflicted injuries rooted in racism. Her large embrace superseded any personal injury she had suffered as a girl or young woman. *Primer for Blacks* was a call to unity—to the strength in numbers. To be black has been defined as having "one drop" of black blood. Gwendolyn embraced those people. Historically, differences in color had been used to divide black people. Now, Gwendolyn said, our differences must be celebrated and validated as one people and a political force.

Also in *Primer for Blacks* is the memorable celebration "To Those of My Sisters Who Kept Their Naturals."

> Never to look
> a hot comb in the teeth.

> *Sisters!*
> *I love you.*
> *Because you love you.*
> *Because you are erect.*
> *Because you are also bent.*

In season, stern, kind.
Crisp, soft—in season.
And you withhold.
And you extend.
And you Step out.
And you go back.
And you extend again.
Your eyes, loud-soft, with crying and with smiles,
are older than a million years.
And they are young.
You reach, in season.
You subside, in season.
And ALL
Below the richrough righttime of your hair.

You have not bought Blondine.
You have not hailed the hot-comb recently.
You never worshipped Marilyn Monroe.
You say: Farrah's hair is hers.
You have not wanted to be white.
Nor have you testified to adoration of that state
with the advertisement of imitation
(never successful because the hot-comb is
laughing too.)

But oh the rough dark Other music!
the Real,
the Right.
The natural Respect of Self and Seal!
Sisters!
Your hair is Celebration in the world!

In the late 1970s, the sea of afros ebbed into relaxed and straightened hair. The majority of black women again turned their backs on their natural beauty. Gwendolyn spoke out against the backtracking and affirmed afros and natural hair styles as statements of identity and pride. She lifted her words in an elegant song against the winds of retrenchment.

These aesthetic concerns remain timely. Unfortunately, the issue of violence inside the black community remains topical as well. And Gwendolyn Brooks turned her attention to bloodshed.

In "The Boy Died in My Alley" (from *Beckonings*, 1975), she ostensibly offers unvarnished testimony of her reaction to the murder of a young neighborhood boy.

> *The Boy died in my alley*
> *Without my having known.*
> *Policeman said, next morning,*
> *"Apparently died Alone."*
>
> *"You heard a shot?" Policeman said.*
> *Shots I hear and Shots I hear.*
> *I never see the dead.*
>
> *The Shot that killed him yes I heard*
> *as I heard the Thousand shots before;*
> *careening tinnily down the nights*
> *across my years and arteries.*
>
> . . .
>
> *I joined the Wild and killed him*
> *with knowledgeable unknowing.*
> *I saw where he was going.*
> *I saw him Crossed. And seeing,*
> *I did not take him down.*
>
> *He cried not only "Father!"*
> *but "Mother!*
> *Sister!*

Brother."
The cry climbed up the alley.
It went up to the wind.
It hung upon the heaven
for a long
stretch-strain of Moment.

The red floor of my alley
Is a special speech to me.

The rarely anthologized poem, here excerpted, is important for three reasons: One, in it, Gwendolyn does not stand as the poet but responds as a woman in a community, as drylongso herself, the everyday black person. Or so it would seem. Two, the poet does not decorate her diction but uses rather ordinary speech, the language of the everyday. Three, Gwendolyn addresses a crucial social issue that is still, unfortunately, at a critical point—black fratricide. "The Boy Died in My Alley" resonates today. Even more so than it did at the time it was written. Gwendolyn was a poet who spoke on matters timely and timeless.

It is difficult to ascertain how Gwendolyn managed to create so healthy a body of work. She spent an enormous amount of time on the road, fulfilling reading engagements. In one month, she had nine engagements in other cities because she needed to support herself and others and to give to her designated worthy young people and causes. In 1981, Gwendolyn read in Illinois, Michigan, Pennsylvania, North Carolina, Iowa, Massachusetts, Connecticut, Indiana, California, New York, District of Columbia, New Jersey, Ohio, Florida, Minnesota, Texas, and Virginia. Sometimes she read more than once in one state. Her readings occurred most often during the academic year, as she was often called to read at schools. She kept her booking agent, Beryl Zitch, very busy arranging her travel and appearances. The year 1982 was especially difficult, as Henry had a heart attack in February, while

Gwendolyn was away giving a reading, and then a stroke in March. Even with family worries, the poet still had to do the work of performance. To be in her audience was to enjoy the proud, black, affirming messages, rich humanity, music, and expression of a master poet. Her audiences were inspired.

She stayed contemporary. She gave each reading her all. She left those in attendance spellbound. And after each reading, she spent time signing her books. As long as there were people with books to sign, Gwendolyn signed them and talked to people about their writing. Long after her readings were concluded, she gave of herself. It was during the summers that Gwendolyn finally got the chance to stay off the traveling train or bus and enjoy her home and quiet writing space. Every writer needs not just a room of her own, but some time alone, too.

Before America had an official poet laureate, the functions of that office were performed by the poetry consultant to the Library of Congress. Gwendolyn Brooks became the twenty-ninth poetry consultant.

Her tenure at the Library of Congress was a success; she defined the work of the poet laureate. She was an activist poetry consultant, welcoming people from the surrounding area to the library, even instituting informal brown-bag readings at lunchtime. Her Mondays and Tuesdays were filled with activities from nine in the morning until deep into the night. Wednesdays she played catch-up, answering correspondence and welcoming guests. She saw visitors from Latin America, Eastern Europe, the Middle East, and one from Africa.

She was ably assisted by a team of librarians from the consultant's office. Their efficiency, which she greatly valued, and warmth not only sustained Gwendolyn for that period but the friendship of some of them lasted through the years in correspondence. These were John Broderick, Nancy Galbraith, Daniel Boorstin, and Jenny Rutland. She describes the library and poetry staff: "Semi-saint John Broderick, assistant librarian for research services, has labored mightily and graciously to get the people here whom I wanted to introduce to you. Cheery, expert cooperative, friendly, self-effacing, John 'Communications' Sullivan! Poetry associate Nancy Galbraith—not only brilliant and knowledgeable in an assortment of areas, but the magnificent wheel-oiler. Upstairs . . . Jenny Rutland, our second poetry associate—new-penny bright, reliable, hard-working, genial and generous."[12] Gwendolyn found the vast Library of Congress warm and welcoming, filled with smiling people, researchers, clerks, pages.

Once her assistants had gotten her in touch with the poets and writers she had selected to read under the bright lights in the dark, solemn Coolidge Auditorium, Gwendolyn had only to write an introduction for each. Then she would present said poet or writer to the attentive crowd gathered. Needless to say, her introductions were little poems about each reader.

In the course of the year, she called forth celebrated writers like James Baldwin, Joyce Carol Oates, William Golding, Doris Grumbach, Keri Hulme, Yevgeny Yevtushenko, Haki Madhubuti, Grace Schuman, Louis Simpson, Michael Harper, Sonia Sanchez, Mari Evans, Michael Anania, Garrison Keillor, David Ignatow, Donald Hall, Sandra Cisneros, Galway Kinnell, and Barbara Guest. And she presented less well known, at the time, poets and writers: Luis Omar Salinas, Alberto Rios, Lorna Dee Cervantes, Etheridge Knight, Kofi Awoonor, Patricia McConel, Les Murray, W. D. Wetherell, John Tagliabue, Michael Benedict, and a very grateful Angela Jackson.

Not only did Gwendolyn present this multicultural array of poets and writers. She also took her poetry to the schools and colleges of DC, Virginia, and Maryland. And she read and led workshops at the Maryland Correctional Facility and Lorton Prison in Virginia.

Gwendolyn's visits to schools and prisons did not begin with her poetry consultancy. She had for many years been visiting these institutions. In addition, in Chicago she made annual visits to Cook County Hospital, where she gave a reading to patients and employees in the auditorium there. Later she read at the bedsides of bed-bound patients. These kind acts were a part of her identity and had been cultivated in her upbringing.

Gwendolyn carried her personality and habits into the office of the poetry consultant of the Library of Congress. Besides her standards of long hours and hard work, Gwendolyn changed the faces of the poets and writers she presented. Before the word "diversity" was fashionable, her reading series was diverse in racial, cultural, and stylistic composition. This intensely literate and humane poet lifted up the face of the real America.

CHAPTER NINE

Blacks

In the decade and a half after her 1985–1986 year as the poetry consultant for the Library of Congress, in which she transformed that office, Gwendolyn continued to keep her promise to be "a voice and speaking eyes" and to "prevail against the editors of the world." She trained her garden well, and she planted and tended widely. She offered poetic sacrament and a seal of approval. She never let up.

Gwendolyn maintained a strenuous reading schedule, traveling by train from California to Connecticut and farther. She continued to give gifts and to support black publishing houses such as Third World Press. She had published her own work in 1980, *Primer for Blacks* (Black Position Press) and *Young Poet's Primer* (Brooks Press). In 1986, she instituted the David Company, named after her father, which would publish her work in a more significant and autonomous way.

In addition, Gwendolyn would reassert her relationship to young people as a teacher, a task she had given up in 1971 after having a mild heart attack while teaching at the City College of New York. Thus, she would give her validation to another generation.

In a letter from January 4, 1987, Gwendolyn wrote to Haki Madhubuti a response to a letter that some black writers were circulating in protest of a major literary award that excluded black recipients. She said,

> Think of all the estimable Blacks who did not receive the "Major" awards. W. E. B. Du Bois, Richard Wright, Zora Neale Hurston, Langston Hughes, James Weldon Johnson, Robert Hayden, James Baldwin. Not a one of them wept. Not a one of them, in the rage of neglect, turned on their Black mates. . . . Can't we carry some dignity? Must we announce to white writers and judges how golden we consider them, . . . and in the same gasp, announce how small we consider ourselves and our own?

Some might say that Gwendolyn had herself received sufficient recognition in major literary awards to downplay their importance to a starving artist. But her message was deeper. She asked of herself and her brother and sister writers a deep dignity that affords self-validation. Gwendolyn herself had been validated at home by encouraging parents who recognized and fed her gift. Early on, she had been able to validate herself as a poet. Then part of her life mission was to validate the dignity and worth of her people. And she validated young writers. Soon she did not ask for prizes; she gave them.

When Gwendolyn Brooks Junior High School opened in Harvey, Illinois, November 24, 1981, its principal reached out to its model, then the poet laureate of Illinois. There developed a friendship centered on the futures, well-being, and academic excellence of the student body. Betty J. Owens regularly sent Gwendolyn newsletters from the school, *The Brooks Courier*, detailing notices for students and parents and extolling the achievements of high-performing honor roll students and achievers in other areas. Gwendolyn, in turn, was known to visit the school. She sponsored an essay contest and bestowed her usual monetary awards. And she sent to Betty Owens a hardcover book for the school library. In June 1987, Gwendolyn requested the names of students who won contests. "Three winning manuscripts and the name of the student who won the $100 award for Best Use of the Library." She signed this missive to Owens: "Love, Gwen Brooks."[1] She was affectionate in that way, and her interest in her namesake school was personal.

On October 5, 1988, the school celebrated Gwendolyn Brooks Day with an open house. Principal Owens reported on the event in *The Brooks Courier*:

> Open House . . . proved to be a very exciting occasion. We were honored with the presence of two outstanding Black female humanitarians, our own Gwendolyn Brooks, poet laureate of the state of Illinois, and Dr. Margaret Burroughs, founder of the DuSable Museum. We unveiled a beautiful oil portrait of Ms. Brooks. Dr. Burroughs, a lifetime acquaintance, made a personal presentation to Gwendolyn Brooks, and a special presentation, a collection of Black prints, to the school in honor of Ms. Brooks.[2]

Gwendolyn signed the program, "With continuing love and pride! Sincerely, Gwendolyn Brooks."

Just as Gwendolyn offered encouragement to the black student body of Harvey, she also gave courage to young people in the Bantustans of South Africa, a half a world away. In *The Near-Johannesburg Boy and Other Poems*, from 1986, published by the David Company and dedicated to the students of Gwendolyn Brooks Junior High School in Harvey, Illinois, she spoke to the similarity of Harvey and Soweto. She takes on the voice of a black boy in the middle of the uprising of his people, as she had close knowledge of the struggle of the South African people from her friend the revolutionary and poet Keorapetse Kgositsile. The elder black woman poet dared to take up the weapon of her voice and use it to speak for and as the young, the black, the defiant, and the self-determining.

In her introduction to the poem "The Near-Johannesburg Boy," Gwendolyn acknowledges that she is speaking for a young person of perhaps Soweto, a black township near Johannesburg. Soweto was the site of a series of furious student uprisings beginning June 16, 1976, in protest of the mandatory use of the oppressors' language, Afrikaans, in the education of the black students, the original and dispossessed people of South Africa. In this poem, Gwendolyn is a member of the profound uprising wherein hundreds of young black people throwing stones were killed by automatic-weapon-wielding white South African policemen.

> In South Africa the Black
> children ask each other
> "Have you been detained yet?
> How many times have you been
> detained?"
> . . .
> The herein boy does not live
> In Johannesburg. He is not
> allowed to live there. Perhaps
> he lives in Soweto.

> *My way is from woe to wonder.*
> *A Black boy near Johannesburg, hot*
> *in the Hot Time.*

> *Those people*
> *do not like Black among the colors.*
> *They do not like our*
> *calling our country ours.*
> *They say our country is not ours.*

> *Those people.*
> *Visiting the world as I visit the world.*
> *Those people.*
> *Their bleach is puckered and cruel.*

It is work to speak of my Father. My Father,
His body was whole till they Stopped it.
Suddenly.
With a short shot.
But, before that, physically tall and among us,
he died every day. Every moment.
My Father . . .
First was the crumpling.
No. First was the Fist-and-the-Fury.
Last was the crumpling. It is
a little used rag that is Under, it is not
it is not my Father gone down.

About my Mother. My Mother
was this loud laugher
below the sunshine, below the starlight at festival.
My mother is still this loud laugher!
Still moving straight in the Getting-It-Done (as she names it.)
Oh the strong eye is my Mother.
Except when it seems we are lax in our looking.

Well, enough of slump, enough of Old Story.
Like a clean spear of fire
I am moving. I am not still. I am ready
to be ready.
I shall flail
In the Hot Time.

Tonight I walk with
a hundred of playmates to where
the hurt Black of our skin is forbidden.
There, in the dark that is our dark, there
a pulse across earth that is our earth, there

there exulting, there Exactly, there redeeming, there
    Roaring Up
(oh my Father)
we shall forge with the Fist-and-the-Fury:
we shall flail in the Hot Time:
we shall
we shall

With deceptive and powerful poetic strokes, Gwendolyn addresses the immorality and cruelty of apartheid and the historical fight of black people for their homeland. She embraces the strength and importance of the black family, which she believes is the foundation for our continuity and struggle. Most significantly, she, in the voice of a young man, takes up whatever arms are at hand.

Gwendolyn's attention had already turned to South Africa in "Music for Martyrs," dedicated to Steve Biko, a student activist and hero of the Black Consciousness movement of South Africa who died in detention in September 1977. "Music for Martyrs" is in "To the Diaspora," a section in the 1981 collection *to disembark*.

The Near-Johannesburg Boy includes poems dedicated to civil rights leader Whitney Young and Haki Madhubuti. It concludes with the sublime and underappreciated "Infirm," which sings that each of us is beautiful and flawed, but beautiful no less. Suffice to say, it sums up Gwendolyn's philosophy in a few short lines.

For her seventieth birthday, Gwendolyn, as poet laureate, gave awards to seventy poets at an event held at the University of Chicago. There were the usual young and gifted school children of elementary and high schools, and there were thirty-two promising, emerging, and established adult voices on the state's poetry scene. These included Sterling Plumpp, Eileen Cherry (Chandler), Reginald Gibbons, Haki Madhubuti, Carolyn Rodgers, Sandra Jackson (Opoku), Michael Anania, Walter Bradford, S. Brandi Barnes, David Hernandez, Paul Hoover, Lisel Mueller, Maxine Chernoff, John Frederick Nims, Eugene Redmond, and Melvin E.

Lewis, as well as to me, Angela Jackson, and to Brooks's husband, Henry Blakely, a gifted and underappreciated poet.

It was a bright, spring day—June 7, 1987—a good day for poets to be celebrated by a revered poet. There was a great deal of appreciative laughter and good cheer. Gwendolyn set the joyous tone with Nora as her assistant; she was witty and applauding at once. The poets celebrated each other. The room at the university was filled with light. Everyone there was a poet or someone who loved a poet and poetry. Gwendolyn was Queen of Poetry. Queen of the day.

One night Gwendolyn's small frame house was burglarized. Alone, she called Haki Madhubuti. With Henry not yet at home, Gwendolyn had sought the protection of her cultural, adopted son.

After he received her harried call, he told her to call 911, and he got dressed. He hid two weapons on his person just in case he met trouble, then jumped in his car and floored the pedal. Madhubuti drove through every red light on East Seventy-Fifth Street between his place and the Blakely house on Evans. By the time he reached the house, the police were already there. As he fast-stepped up the walk, they moved toward him. Gwendolyn came out on the porch and exclaimed, "That's my son!" to stop the police. Madhubuti thought, "So I'm her son." He understood who he was to her then.

He went into her bedroom and stashed his two "pieces" under her bed.

After the burglary, Gwendolyn did not feel safe in the old neighborhood and decided to look elsewhere. On January 22, 1991, Gwendolyn Brooks purchased a cooperative apartment at 5530 South Shore Drive, in Hyde Park. She and Henry moved in shortly thereafter. It would be their last residence.

Before the momentous move to Hyde Park from the house on Evans Avenue, where the Blakelys had lived for more than twenty years, Gwendolyn Brooks had gone back to teaching.

Chicago State University grew from a nineteenth-century normal, or teaching, school. After several name and curriculum changes, as well as changes in student composition, the name of the institution became, in 1971, Chicago State University. In 1972, the university moved to a newly built complex at Ninety-Fifth and King Drive. By 1980, 80 percent of the student body was African American and were of limited means.

Madhubuti invited Gwendolyn to Chicago State University, offering her a distinguished chair at an excellent salary. She would be required to give one reading a year. Gwendolyn refused. She would only take on the position if it required something more of her. She chose to teach one poetry workshop class in the spring of each year. Truly, the incentive that lured Gwendolyn out of teaching retirement to Chicago State was not the title or the salary that came with it. It was the composition of the student body that moved her. When Madhubuti told her that a high percentage of the student body was working black women, that excited her even more.

These working black women students were whom she had been as a student at Woodrow Wilson Junior College in the 1930s. She knew what they needed, and she felt a sense of responsibility to them. "Duty" was not an ugly word to Gwendolyn. It was a part of black consciousness and social conscience and an empathetic core. Not to be discounted was her Christian upbringing under the wings of David and Keziah Brooks.

This concern for others was not limited to students. Her care for children was demonstrated in not only the ideal *Bronzeville Boys and Girls* but also the socially aware *Children Coming Home* (The David Company, 1991). In *Children Coming Home*, Gwendolyn deals with a wide range of topics, from naming identity and neglect to sexual molestation, as in "Uncle Seagram." She was as much a mother as a poet. Her maternal instincts were so developed, she nurtured, encouraged, and addressed children whenever possible. Her care was extensive and exhaustive.

She expressed to Madhubuti, in a letter dated December 29, 1993, her commitment to her own care and health by spending "January in the house writing my 10,000 speech." She went on to make further resolutions to safeguard herself. "My plans for the future Haki are these." She planned to write at least two more books, to travel for readings, to attend his classes at CSU, and all the other required meetings and graduations. Socially, she allocated for herself a yearly movie and biannual attendance at a play. She was strict with herself when she pledged to regularize her sleeping patterns and continue to stay in her apartment all of July and August, "writing without interruptions from outdoors." She swore off all parties that were not work related. She was seventy-six years old and the press of mortality was upon her. Her mother had lived to be ninety years old. Gwendolyn ended her letter to Madhubuti with a quote. "One of my favorite guides taken dozens of years ago from a TV documentary . . . 'Swan runs *his* life. He doesn't just trot along after it.'"

The primary importance of this letter of resolutions is its sense of self-determination. She was choosing the course of herself for herself. This kind of choosing in the democratic political arena is the vote of each citizen. We must recall that Gwendolyn was a woman who had already had a mild heart attack. She knew that the body had an expiration date. And she determined to own the life that she had and to take care of it. She gave of herself so wholeheartedly in public (and in her letter writing) that she had to protect her privacy fiercely.

Gwendolyn voiced her choice of Harold Washington for mayor of Chicago in 1983 and again in 1987. She praised him in the poem "Harold Washington." He was the first black mayor of that city and in his way a forerunner of President Barack Obama.[3] In another more oppressive arena, it is the choice to resist or engage in revolution as in "The Near-Johannesburg Boy." Citizen Brooks recognized that the basis of her action in her community was as a self-determining individual. She recognized further that her community in its entirety must be self-determining.

She allowed no intrusion on her privacy, sometimes not answering the phone. When her friend Val Gray Ward called her but got no response, she knew, as Madhubuti knew and as Gwendolyn's family knew, that she was more than likely occupied with her soap operas, like millions of other black women. Or that Gwendolyn simply did not wish to be disturbed. She was just like regular folks. (When she gave a reading at St. Xavier College in Chicago in 1969, my own sister Rose likes to tell the story of how they talked about the soaps over lunch.)

And not everyone had Gwendolyn's phone number. Only a chosen few. Ward was her longtime friend in the struggle. When Gwendolyn was unable to meet an engagement because of a family emergency, Ward substituted for her. Ward's Kuumba Theater honored Miss Brooks with its Kuumba Liberation Award, and Gwendolyn supported Kuumba in its drives to raise money for Africare and other efforts. In the mid-1990s, Ward and her husband relocated to upstate New York because he had a teaching position there. This did not end the friendship between the two women. They talked on the phone.

And there was Sonia Sanchez. Gwendolyn and Sanchez read together on the black woman for the Nation of Islam and worked together often, as well as enjoying a lively friendship.

The Guild Literary Complex was founded on the North Side of Chicago as a bookstore and center for signings and readings. By 1989, it had evolved into a performance space where musicians played and poets and prose writers performed, their work. The Guild Complex is devoted to diversity, social justice, and cutting-edge work. Soon it became famous for its open-mic readings where young poets might come and share their work. Gwendolyn had known about the Guild from the beginning, but when the open mics were instituted, she generously instituted in 1993 the Gwendolyn Brooks Prize of $500 for poetry.

One young poet, recently arrived from Oklahoma, was Quraysh Ali Lansana. He met Gwendolyn at the Guild Complex in 1993. She encouraged him to return to college to finish his degree and directed him to Chicago State University, where she had begun teaching in 1990.

Also recently arrived in Chicago from Yale University was Emily Hooper, who met Miss Brooks at Columbia College when she was performing Gwendolyn's poem "To the Diaspora." Gwendolyn was so pleased with her performance that they exchanged contact information. The poet told the young actor that her daughter, Nora, had a theater group in which she might be interested.

One evening in July 1993 Lansana came to give Gwendolyn a ride to the Guild Complex. As they approached his car, Gwendolyn was thrilled to see Emily Hooper there. As Lansana helped the poet laureate into the backseat, she looked at him and said of his companion, "I approve."

Hooper was a storyteller and actor, and Lansana a poet and performer. They were a part of a vibrant art scene of a new New Breed. This scene was focused at the Guild Literary Complex and Spices jazz bar, both on the North Side. In a letter dated June 24, 1992, Hooper wrote Gwendolyn seeking permission to direct "The Near-Johannesburg Boy" in a performance piece that included the work of Michael Warr, Rohan Preston, Leon Wilson, Sylvia Carter, Sharon Powell, Angela Shannon, Chris Chill, and Quraysh Ali Lansana. The piece would be performed at Spices. "It is certainly a timely and powerful piece," Hooper wrote. Surely, the idea of her poem being performed in a jazz bar was more than appealing to Gwendolyn. The inclusion of her work by these young poets gave them poetic credibility and approval. Inversely, it kept Gwendolyn young-minded and contemporary. Just as she had mentored the poets of the 1960s, she now mentored the poets of the 1990s.

After Lansana entered Chicago State University to complete his bachelor's degree, he submitted his work for consideration for Gwendolyn's poetry workshop to Dr. Donda West, who was chair of the English Department and mother of a boy who would become a superstar of rap, Kanye West. It was the spring of 1997 and it was the last undergraduate workshop that Gwendolyn would teach. She had considered retiring in 1995, but for some reason had changed her mind. Also in that workshop was Bryant Smith. Lansana and Bryant Smith were the two males in a class of approximately eleven female students. Smith, an English major, had been steered to the workshop by Dr. B. J. Bolden.

When they entered that classroom, Gwendolyn reigned quietly. Bryant Smith describes her as "so small in stature, but a huge presence. She commanded the room with her knowledge and, to be honest, her red pen." Her pen was her scepter and her utensil. She would take their poems home and write in the margins her criticisms, responses, questions. She used her red pen often. "It was basically an intense workshop with this giant of a woman."

Lansana describes her in the classroom as rather like a kindly instigator. "She would throw out ideas for us to consider, then sit back and rub her hands and just grin with a mischievous grin. . . . She just sat back and enjoyed the conversation. . . . I remember her egging us on, pushing, prodding, pushing ideas, pushing us to think."

She offered them prompts, newspaper articles to write on or about. She assigned a form as well, a sestina or sonnet. She asked them to find "found poems," that took them "outside." Bryant Smith says, "She would give us words or phrases and tell us to write about them. . . . She shot me into the stratosphere of carving poems out of words instead of using clichés. . . . During first semester, she took us to dinner to soak up the experience of writers enjoying a meal together. She took us to the mansion on 111th, a high-end soul-food place. At least once a year she wanted to continue that. She exposed me to places that I never even thought to try."

When they chose the place and took her to the Shark Bar, she ordered a pork chop and did not care for it. "We surprised her and paid for it." At last, a group of students who were attentive to her needs, who reciprocated. Of that last class, only one or two students left the class. Bryant Smith says they "had life challenges and fell away." Gwendolyn kept students by the power of her personality and intellect.

In 1990, Haki Madhubuti had brought Gwendolyn to Chicago State University with an endowed chair. He also had instituted the Gwendolyn Brooks Center for Black Literature and Creative Writing and an MFA program in creative writing that was centered on black writing. This Brooks Center gave annual conferences on African American literature and attracted the most esteemed names because of the presence and stature of Gwendolyn Brooks. Some of the poets and writers who came to the annual conference were Toni Morrison, August Wilson, Terry MacMillan, Maya Angelou, Rita Dove, Octavia Butler, Amiri Baraka, Sonia Sanchez, Nikki Giovanni, Mari Evans, Kalamu ya Salaam, Lucille Clifton, Dr. Houston Baker, Dr. Eleanor Traylor, and Dr. Eugene Redmond.

One memorable moment from those conferences was one in which Maya Angelou was featured. Lansana describes how Maya Angelou came in "just after her brother died. Maya was staying with Oprah. Oprah put her in her limo. The limo pulled up in back of Robinson Center [on the CSU campus]. Maya did a twenty-five to thirty minute medley of poems from the Harlem Renaissance to Miss Brooks. The interaction from Miss Brooks, the concern, the comfort, the love that Miss Brooks showed Miss Maya. That was a memorable moment from the conference."

Another heartfelt moment was "Miss Brooks and Mama Lucille [Clifton]. Mama Lucille had just recovered from one of her many battles with cancer. She talked about it and read about it, and everyone in the audience was weeping. Miss Brooks was comforting to Miss Lucille."

On the other hand, "Watching Dr. [Eleanor] Traylor and Miss Brooks was always fun. Dr. Traylor was always protective, always doting." As was Sonia Sanchez. As was Madhubuti.

The Jefferson Lectures in the Humanities was begun in 1972 as an honorary series by the National Endowment for the Humanities and is the federal government's highest honor for intellectual achievement in the humanities. On May 4, 1994, Gwendolyn Brooks delivered the Jefferson Lecture at the Kennedy Center Concert Hall, Washington, DC, before an audience of approximately 2,300.

The lecture was a wide-ranging, keen-minded address of scattershots and explorations. She called the speech "Family Pictures" after the title of her book and said that the "Family therein referred to is Blackness."[4]

She began with a naming of names of characters from her poetry and prose. She called them her "Gallery" and identified them with lines from her poetry: Satin-Legs Smith, Sadie and Maud, Old Black Woman, Homeless and Indistinct; Malcolm, Lil Ms. Entrepreneur, Pearl May Lee, the mother of Emmett Till, Winnie Mandela, Langston Hughes, Paul Robeson, a Garbageman, and many, many more comprising blackness. She said, "Blackness is what I know best." But she also said, as she had said to an audience of whites in 1951, "We know the condition of your gums because we have been so long between your teeth."[5] Whoever said Gwendolyn Brooks was not a truth-teller before it was fashionable to tell the truth in outspoken ways?

Gwendolyn ably handled the exploration of identity, on blackness, and Americanness. We are "operationally" American, she said. She learned from travel outside the country. But she embraced a big family of blackness that is global.

Hers was not only a lecture about identity and familyhood. It also took a stand on values. Gwendolyn reminded us that she was familiar with Russian literature and had read long hours on the traveling train from reading to reading.

One person she read of was the politician Vladimir Zhirinovsky, who hated the idea of "all these Blacks" running around in this country with "all this Power." Gwendolyn found Zhirinovsky abhorrent and said of him,

I am sure that one of Zhirinovsky's admirations is Niccolo Machiavelli, author of *The Prince*. Surely Zhirinovsky squealed and dampened himself when he read "A Prince should disregard the reproach of being thought cruel when it enables him to keep his Subjects united and obedient." Surely it was a while before Z was dry. And likely he was again visited by difficulties when he went on to read: "Fortune is a woman, who, to be kept under, must be beaten and roughly handled; and we see that she suffers herself to be more readily mastered by those who so treat her than by those who are more timid in their approach."

She did not take to people just because they were important.

It was clear where Gwendolyn's values rested. If she be a queen, she was a queen of kindness and generosity. As a woman, she cast her lot with other women: women were to be treated with equality and respect. She made her point clear by her bitter bite, her slicing sarcasm.

She asked of her black community, her family, the kind of collective action taken to elect Harold Washington mayor of Chicago. She was still proud of that united action, the success. She believed that "lots of littles" can move mountains.

And she was humble. Gwendolyn had been to the White House at the Scholars' Reception when Lyndon B. Johnson was president. She had stood tongue-tied before his smiling countenance. Lady Bird she found warm and gracious. But in the end, she broke protocol: she left before the presidential party. Sometimes she got in a mood where she just had to leave. But the second time she visited the White House was more comfortable. It was on October 5, 1995, when she received the National Medal of the Arts from President William Jefferson Clinton. She was small and demure and smiling.

Her eightieth birthday celebration, on June 7, 1997, at the Harold Washington Library, was a big splash. A bank of lights flooded the stage in the auditorium. Poets and writers came from near and far to honor her. Civic leaders and personalities all gathered to praise her. It was a highlight in the cultural calendar of the city that loved her.

In 1996, *Report from Part Two* was published by Third World Press. In it, Gwendolyn continued her life story. Certain parts of the story she looked at again. She looked at Henry L. Blakely Jr., her husband, again and found him good. She remembered his belief in her work, so strong that he urged her to place it before any housewifery. She remembered the physical vitality of the man who in their youth could push any of their old, broken cars to where it needed to go. She celebrated the fact that they would soon be celebrating fifty-six years of marriage.

Henry unfortunately passed away in his sleep at the Blakelys' home near Lake Michigan in Hyde Park on July 3, 1996. Born on November

27, 1916, he was seventy-nine years old. Henry was called "the Poet of Sixty-Third Street," calling up those important creative years when he and Gwendolyn had resided on that historic thoroughfare. His well-regarded volume of poetry, *Windy Place*, was published in 1974 by Broadside Press, a year after he and Gwendolyn reunited and the year they traveled to Ghana together. He was at work on another book of poems and a novel, as well as essays on black development called *The Sectorplan*. He was a founder of a group of black writers, the Perspectivists. His philosophy of writing was that poets must "make entries into the larger record, entries that further selfhood and additionally identify a people and time to other people and times."

When Gwendolyn was a young woman, she had looked up at a young man standing in a doorway and knew a good part of her life would be shared with him. After Henry passed away, the family and some friends memorialized him at an eightieth birthday party at the Whitehall. It was an unusual tribute, conceived by a family of a poet. Margaret Burroughs wrote Gwendolyn that Henry would have loved the gathering "in absentia." Dr. Burroughs had been widowed as well, and Gwendolyn and Henry had offered her comfort and support for the DuSable Museum. Now Dr. Burroughs offered Gwendolyn the comfort of an "old acquaintance."

Gwendolyn was shaken by Henry's death. Her voice turned downcast and weary by another event. She called Nora, Madhubuti, and Lansana to ask them what to do. She had hired a cleaning service to come in and help her clean her storage area in her condo. She needed to thin out the mass of paper, clippings, stacks of notebooks, lesson plans, journals, recipes, photographs, and lots of correspondence in her storage room. But these helpers made off with boxes of Gwendolyn's intellectual property. They took the boxes to a rare books dealer, who put them on the market. Somewhere in the midst of their cleaning, they had awakened to the fact that this little old lady was Somebody and might be worth something.

Gwendolyn received a call from the Bancroft Library at the University of California at Berkeley in the spring of 1999 offering her ten thousand dollars for her archive. Gwendolyn had not intended for anyone to have her papers yet. But the Bancroft Library would have her property whether she took the money or not. The whole process was legal. Not right, but legal. Gwendolyn was advised to take the money. She did. The Bancroft Library celebrated its acquisition.

She continued to give readings even after her booking agent and close friend Beryl Zitch of Contemporary Forum passed away from cancer in 1998. Beryl had been Gwendolyn's champion, seeking out and arranging her readings, making sure that all her travel was smoothed over and her hotel lodgings amenable. Like Henry, Beryl had celebrated her every victory and commendation. Gwendolyn carried on without her, ever the professional. She made notes on her contracts of special poems to read or the order of her readings. Even after turning eighty, she continued her habit of giving full readings and following these with book signings and conversations with audience members long after the readings were over. She talked to people, gave encouragement to writers, and listened until the last person had been met. Her energy and interest was unwavering. She was an indefatigable and dignified lover of humanity.

One afternoon in August of 2000, Quraysh Ali Lansana, his wife, Emily Hooper Lansana, and their two young toddler sons came to say good-bye to Miss Brooks. She had written a recommendation for Quraysh and he was about to study for his MFA at New York University. Emily corralled the two rambunctious boys so they would not wreak havoc in the Blakely apartment. Gwendolyn, Emily, and the boys sat smiling while Quraysh took an emblematic picture of the happiness of the Great Poet with the little ones she loved so well, her godchildren. It was a day that shone with joy. They remembered how when their son Nile was a month old and his father was carrying him awkwardly, Gwendolyn had said, "Stop carrying that baby like a football." Precious memories.

Her life was all that it had been and more. Years before she and her son, Hank, had been distant. Now they were together. They talked.

They shared so many good memories. She enjoyed her grandson, Nicholas, and Hank's wife, Lillian Christman.

Gwendolyn traveled and gave her readings up until a month before her time. Then she retired to her condominium apartment on the lake. The lake could not have been blue, more a gray-like stone, unyielding, the water heavy.

Gwendolyn was not fond of doctors and rarely sought them out. Nora and Haki Madhubuti took her to the University of Chicago Hospital and Medical Center, but they said that it was too late. The cancer was too far gone. It was a week before her time.

Dr. Jizunga Wright took care of her at home visitations. Nora brought her medicine. She and Madhubuti put her in a hospital bed. They made her as comfortable as she could be when her body was filled with so much suffering. The cancer was excruciating. Her mind would not rest. She wandered inside. When Quraysh called her from New York and identified himself, she said, "Who?" Her voice was curt, cutting with pain.

That Sunday, December 4, 2000, they gathered in her rooms, family and close friends, visiting throughout the day. Her body moved inexorably toward its end. They turned her hospital bed toward the east window. They read to her from her works throughout the day. They read her elegant words. Madhubuti and his wife, Safisha, and always Nora. They watched over her.

Madhubuti, her cultural son, stood on one side and Nora, her daughter, stood on the other side of her bed. They took her hands. Nora placed a pen in her hand.

After a time, Gwendolyn Elizabeth Brooks Blakely gave her spirit back to the Spirit. Her pen was still in her hand.

The funeral was on a white day. The city had not seen so heavy a snowfall in many a year. Snow swirled, beat down, drifted, made mountains outside Rockefeller Chapel at 5850 South Woodlawn Avenue, in the heart of the University of Chicago campus, in the middle of the South Side. Mourners were blind with snow and grief as they inched their way into the huge, high-ceilinged chapel.

Poet Elizabeth Alexander trudged through the snow. "I had to come," she told me. She had flown in from out of town. Years before, Gwendolyn Brooks had given her an award, recognizing her literary talent.

People came from all parts of the country to honor this poet and writer of splendid skill and generous heart.

The snow was so heavy it had stopped some of them. They had had to turn back. But the church was full.

The program began with music: "Breaths" by Sweet Honey in the Rock. After a dance and libation, Lerone Bennett, Gwendolyn's longtime friend and fellow activist-writer and historian, officiated the service. Hank, Nora, and Haki Madhubuti each had shared memories and reflections in the printed program along with the obituary. They gave insights into Gwendolyn as mother, woman, and poet. Then, at the podium, there were "Messages from the World," alternating with musical selections. Messages were reflections from Mayor Richard M. Daley; Dr. Margaret Burroughs; poet-playwright-activist Useni Eugene Perkins; and Lois Weisberg, director of the Chicago Office of Fine Arts. Madhubuti gave the eulogy.

Cynthia Walls of Chocolate Chips Theater Company read the many acknowledgements. More music. Then the pallbearers carried the casket out. It was borne to Lincoln Cemetery, 12300 South Kedzie Avenue. After the cortege had wound through the snow-covered streets, people gathered at Chicago State University where Gwendolyn Brooks had long reigned in a surprised queenhood in an enduring black sun.

CHAPTER TEN

Immortality of a Kind

Poets and writers are immortal; they live as long as their words are spoken and speak to people. Because her poems and fiction are so captivating and faithful to the black experience, consequently the human experience, Gwendolyn Brooks will continue to be read and be alive.

Gwendolyn Brooks is immortal because she impacts and influences other poets and writers and others who influence poets and writers and others. Her genius and personality increase exponentially. Teachers taught students who in turn taught students about her work. Often anthologized, "We Real Cool" became one of the most well- known American poems. It is a part of the American heart, or should be, because it is so often taught.

There are lucky people who experienced Gwendolyn and her work personally. They were mothered or mentored by her, befriended by her, taught by her, or heard her read, or got the chance to talk with her after one of her many readings. Haki Madhubuti knew her well; he was her cultural son. After she passed on, he said,

Thirty-three years of a loving familyhood with Gwen and Nora have been an integral part of my life. As cultural mother, serious friend, mentor, God-mother to our daughter, extraordinary encourager and emotional/financial supporter of Third World Press, the Institute of Positive Education and our schools. Meeting her in 1967 was like rain hitting new seeds of corn in an excellent harvest year. She, in her quiet but determined manner, was able to cut into my young cool and turn it warm inviting to the genuine warmth of her personhood. I began to smile.

In 1970, I had truly become a part of her family along with her husband, Henry (a fine poet himself), her daughter, Nora (very creative with a strong interest in children's theater), and her son, Hank, whom I did not meet until later in our relationship. . . . She literally transformed and saved my life.

Gwendolyn Brooks was the first person, artist, poet with national presence that I met who was realistically modest without a self-congratulatory organ in her body, fully aware of her weaknesses and never took herself too seriously.

Yes, it was the poet, artist and her unique dedication to that which was good, just, correct, and right that pulled me into her family. However, I stayed there for over three decades because of the defining characteristics of her wonderful life. As Don L. Lee I had minor fame that was too consuming and I decided in conversations with her and others to change my name to Haki R. Madhubuti (which she was not in full agreement with). Yet she understood the pull that the culture had on me thus restricting me to be as authentic as she and I wanted. With the new name and off the poetic popular grind, I turned my energies toward rebuilding: local institutional structures, completing an MFA in creative writing at the University of Iowa, creation of the GB center at CSU, my family and extended family as well as heightening my teaching and working in local, international, political, cultural activities. Writing my books and publishing the creative works of others remained a passion. Third World Press had become Gwen's primary publisher. We published, in her lifetime, ten of her books and three studies of her work by renowned scholars.

Her attachment to my bones remained nourishing, a friendly daily dose of calcium that allowed the joints in my writing hand to continue on their mission. As was she, my notes to paper into poems, essays, and occasional fiction is the clear mandate that one does not have control over. She left excellent creative baggage with thousands and with me.

she was our kindness
there will be no final words[1]

"During Brooks's lifetime and ever since, Chicago has made it its job to immortalize Gwendolyn Brooks," said Donald G. Evans, founding executive director of the Chicago Literary Hall of Fame. He went on to say the following:

To say Gwendolyn Brooks is a Chicago institution is true not just metaphorically, but literally. Of all the wildly successful and accomplished writers in Chicago's great literary heritage—a heritage that spans nearly a century and a half—Gwendolyn alone permeated the fabric of this city. It would take a determined detective to find more than trace evidence of Saul Bellow, Nelson Algren, Carl Sandburg, Lorraine Hansberry, Ben Hecht, Richard Wright, Edna Ferber, and so on and so forth.

Brooks lived a long time amongst us Chicagoans, and not just as a celebrity. Walk into just about any school or library or cultural center in the greater Chicago area—this, nearly two decades after her death—and you're likely to find somebody with a story, an event poster, a signed book. Listen to students and writers respond to Brooks's poetry, and you'll hear the voices, young and old, of people who've just received a gift, if not an epiphany. This is a case not just of Gwendolyn Brooks touching people, but of people touching her back.

Brooks was one of us—no question about that, at all—but that doesn't quite explain her universal appeal. It starts, probably, with the fact that Brooks, practically speaking, lived and died her whole life in this city, while others came from and left for elsewhere. Her neighborhood was *her* neighborhood; its people *her* people. But more so, I think Brooks embodied what we Chicagoans like to think of ourselves, in our highest estimation. Her boldness never overwhelmed her humility, nor did her humility ever barricade her boldness. Her brutal honesty, especially in her art, was a form—a uniquely Chicago form—of compassion. Her tireless work ethic was purposeful and got results. Her speaking skills were rivaled only by her listening skills, her penchant for being noticed paralleled only by her determination to notice others. And none of that would have mattered one iota had not her literary art been absolutely dazzling—dazzling, again, in a way Chicagoans like to think of themselves: accessible but profound.

For all those reasons, when the Chicago Literary Hall of Fame voted in its inaugural class, the six selectors unanimously and without hesitation put Brooks at the top of the list. Remember, this was the very first class, meaning the selection committee had the whole of Chicago literary history from which to choose. And Gwendolyn Brooks was a no doubter.

Another national institution was impacted by Gwendolyn and her impact began with one person. Toi Derricotte was influenced by Gwendolyn as a woman, a poet, and future mentor to many.

My first book had been published and I was working on my second when I first studied Gwendolyn Brooks with any seriousness. In the late sixties, Pearl London, one of my most influential teachers, read several of her poems in my first poetry workshop at the New School. She spent an hour on "We Real Cool," articulating the intention of every word, punctuation mark, line break, and especially pointing out (for us to emulate) the power of her verbs. And how the music and line breaks underscored the meaning. But it was another poem that Ms. London shared that changed my life, "the mother," an exquisite poem about a woman who has had several abortions.

I was a new poet and had already begun to follow the confessional poets, so I felt at home with a poem that dug into matters, especially matters in women's lives, that were "unspeakable." Even though Ms. London reminded us the use of "I" didn't mean the poem was personal, I saw the subject of Ms. Brooks's poem as a road sign to a place that had previously been blocked. Here was a black woman poet speaking in an intimate way about something that most people, certainly most black people, considered "shameful" and kept in silence.

I had wanted to write about the birth of my son in a home for unwed mothers, but my pregnancy had been so shame-filled for my black middle-class family that my own son had never been told the story of his birth. I was taught that it was up to us to prove that we were not what "they" thought, and often that had meant hiding dirty laundry for generations.

Miss Brooks made me see that a black woman, a black woman poet, would stand with me, that I wouldn't be completely thrown out of the tribe. It was the reaction of my own people that I had most feared.

A few years after, I went to a reading she gave in New York and heard her breathtaking style, unlike any voice I would ever hear. Its unique quality reminded me of another black singer who couldn't be imitated, Billie Holliday. Who could ever read her poems like Gwendolyn Brooks read them? Who I now realize was the first performance poet I ever heard.

After the reading, I waited in a very long line to have her sign her book and, quaking in the presence of such blinding perfection, I bent down to where she was sitting and told her how struck I had been by her poems and voice. Then, insanely, I asked her if I could send her a copy of my first book, which had just been published, and she said yes, putting her address on the same page as her autograph. Was that even possible? I felt as if I had gotten inside of an elevator whose door opened on the Milky Way.

She sent me back a handwritten note, its large black letters casually written—not at all what I expected a great poet's writing to look like. It looked more like a postcard from an aunt with a recipe scribbled on the back. She said how glad she was to have met me, and how she welcomed me as an important writer into the poetry community. She had seen me. I was a daughter.

Reginald Gibbons, poet, novelist, and Distinguished Professor of English and Classics at Northwestern University, gives ideas on why Gwendolyn is so enduring. When I asked him about her impact and influence on him and American poetry, he responded,

My reaction is like that of most people who can read poetry: she was one of the greatest and most important of American poets in the entire twentieth century. She was not only a virtuoso with language and the poetic line, but she was also the kind of poet who can remake herself, in her artistic development over a long life, and create new work that extends her reach. I put her in the same category offered to us by W. B. Yeats, who wrote "The friends that have it I do wrong / Whenever I remake a song / Should know what issue is at stake— / It is myself that I remake." He was speaking of revising a poem, yet Gwendolyn Brooks, like Yeats, also exemplified how the poet can remake the self that experiences and writes, and thus remain open to changing experience and circumstances, and create new ways of portraying the human condition. So I greatly admire her development; and I have my favorite poems that never fail to refresh my feeling and thought, and my sense of language and of poetry. That she was kind enough to befriend me, too, was a great gift. After my novel came out, an acquaintance held a book party for me in an apartment off North Michigan Ave., and when I got to the apartment door, I saw there was a Western Union envelope pinned there, addressed to me. Inside was a telegram from Gwendolyn congratulating me on the book. No one else ever did that, for me! So I felt honored by something even greater than her presence—I would never have expected her to attend, and I don't think I knew that she had been invited. That something greater was her sense of a kind of poetic ethics—she wanted to offer encouragement to so many people, and not only beginners. I don't know anyone else who was ever as generous as she, in that way.

Poet Patricia Spears Jones never met Gwendolyn personally, yet she was informed by her.

When I was a teen I found out there were Black poets—I read *Negro Digest* and *Ebony* and Gwendolyn Brooks was in them or talked about in them. And somewhere along the way I read "The Chicago Defender Sends a Man to Little Rock" and since I grew up in Arkansas, this cemented my desire to find out more about this Black woman poet. I did not grow up in an academic home—many fellow poets are the children of people with personal libraries—but my mother brought home the journals from McCalls and Reader's Digest and Jet and Sepia (oh those tawdry stories) and we subscribed to Ebony. But I walked to Jim Edgar Drugstore and bought copies of Negro Digest that became Black World. I was already seeing how concepts can change by the very titles of journals. I could see how important it was to go from Negro to Black.

Gwendolyn Brooks' long literary life is a model of moving from Negro to Black. But it seems to me, she was Black always. But Black to her was located in a deep faith in the complexity, energy and the struggle for humanity that Black folks developed in wilderness America. And I think that is why she could discuss class in her work. The subtle critiques of the well to do; the aspirations of the middle class; the poor who could be struggling, angry, criminal or despairing, she could see how wilderness America treated us all. I teach "a song in the front yard" which could be read fairly superficially, but it is anything but. The persona in that poem, a young woman desiring to break away from class and status strictures, to explore her sexuality, to not "be a rose" is seen through the persona's fascination with the "charity children" who do not have curfew; who steal; who parade their sexual attractiveness. But it is her dialogue with the mother in the poem—the one who warns, that gives the poem its tart punch. The mother is the protector, not only of morals and her daughter, but of status which may be difficult to attain and sustain. The perspectives on the poor, the status conscious middle, the desire for more all through the prism of Black lives, makes her poetry and her prose a model for us all. Because to me Gwendolyn Brooks' work says of Black people, we are of a large, complex, and important imagined world, and she passed away a celebrated Black woman poet, knowing the charity children, the sexually oppressed, the soldier, the gang banger, the philanthropists from the suburbs, the peace makers, and the warriors among us. She knew the world.

Gwendolyn offered a life line to black women struggling in all settings and situations. One example is educator and community advocate Renee Knox, who looked to Gwendolyn in her academic endeavor as she worked toward her doctorate and outside the academic setting.

One factor that has helped me to persevere in life is my early exposure to the influence of Gwendolyn Brooks. Although I was not a poet, her perceptive legacy made me proud of my heritage. Her work often spoke to our ability to triumph in the face of obstacles.

By standing on both her, as well as mentees of her, shoulders, in my higher educational pursuits, [that] gave me courage to keep my voice in a system that tried to silence my sentiments that black women were worthy of recognition. Her work also confirmed my belief that uplifting black women did not diminish black men but ascertained the need for male-female relationships for our mutual survival.

Distinct though it is, Gwendolyn's voice has given rise to thousands of voices because her words urge us to speak and do. Parneshia Jones, poet and poetry editor at Northwestern University Press, says, as a foremother,

> Gwendolyn Brooks is a literary and cultural essential. Her work, absolute and opulent, is archetype in revealing how we move around in those tight kitchenette spaces and feelings where often we are unsure, but we must survive. From the streets in Bronzeville to the stacks of the Library of Congress, Brooks reflected community, allowing herself to be vessel and voice to the untitled, the overlooked, and the restricted. Her undeniable creative risks and poetic empathy and elegance represent one of the finest exhibitions of literary excellence in American letters.

I, myself, first met Miss Brooks when I was a young collegiate member of the OBAC Writers Workshop. She was "Miss Brooks" to me. There was a hush in my voice when I said it, for I knew she was a great poet and I felt awe in her presence, delight and wonder before her words. What there was to know about the mysteries of language I learned in the main from this master poet—with some Zora Neale Hurston, some ironic Mari Evans—some everybody black. But mostly I learned the deft turns of Gwendolyn Brooks and turned them around until they were mine. She would not have wanted me to copy her. Who likes a copycat? She herself said that I was an "experimenter" and like no one else. I treasure her assessment. She herself was an experimenter and like no one else. She passed to us her regard for technique and technical daring. She liked it when the Black Arts poets did new things. She admired Haki Madhubuti's craft and constant growth as an artist. His work and his person received a special blessing because he was also serious as an activist and institution builder. She understood the importance of black institutions and felt it was her responsibility to support them.

Poet and children's advocate Useni Eugene Perkins sees Brooks as a bridge.

> As a writer who bridged both the Black Chicago Renaissance (1935–1955) and the Black Arts Movement (1960–1975), I was privileged to discern Gwendolyn Brooks's indelible influence on both of these historic periods. In doing so, although her celebrity was nurtured during the Black Chicago Renaissance, she became a literary icon and mentor to many of the writers who began to develop during the Black Arts Movement. Her dedication to her craft and unwavering commitment to young writers will always be remembered as the hallmarks of her extraordinary literary career.

She was honored in her lifetime and beyond.

In Chicago on 111th Street is the site of Gwendolyn Brooks College Preparatory Academy. It is a spacious campus with the buildings set back from the street. In Harvey, Illinois, is situated Gwendolyn Brooks Middle School. Other schools named after Brooks are in Aurora, Bolingbrook, Eola, and Oak Park. In the early 1970s, Western Illinois University opened a very active Gwendolyn Brooks Cultural Center, where she often read. In her lifetime, she received more than seventy honorary degrees from around the country. A small Chicago park was named after her. Her name, among several, is engraved on the Carter G. Woodson Regional Library in Chicago. Her name is also engraved on the Illinois State Library in Springfield. She has been honored with a postage stamp. A plaque has been placed in front of her Evans home.

But these honors are physical appreciations and no match for the spiritual continuance of her legacy in the lives of others. For this reason, poets celebrate her each year on her birthday, June 7. The annual celebration—known as Brooksday—was conceived by Northwestern University professor Reginald Gibbons in 2013. A day-long presentation of the poet laureate's work takes place at the Chicago Cultural Center and the Logan Center at the University of Chicago. Each year, the event is filled with readers young and old and audience members young and old. Every year, attendance grows.

Legendary Black Arts poet Sonia Sanchez describes Gwendolyn as "a brave warrior woman" who taught her how "to be a person with young people. . . . She taught me you can't get tired until you've signed the last person's book. . . . She was generous. I learned that from her. I don't care how little you have. You make sure that the younger people have some." Brooks taught others dedication to the young.

Kevin Coval is the artistic director of Young Chicago Authors and founder of Louder Than a Bomb: The Chicago Youth Poetry Festival. He appreciates the influence Gwendolyn's work has had on current popular culture, especially music.

> Ms. Brooks sits in the crown of the culture, of hip-hop and breakbeat poetic practice. She is our matriarch. If not for her, no us. No BreakBeat Poets, no "Louder Than a Bomb." We tell it like this: Ms. Brooks begat The Black Arts Poets, Haki Madhubuti, Angela Jackson, Carolyn Rodgers who begat The Last Poets & The Watts Prophets & Gil Scott Heron, who begat Coke La Rock, Melle Mel, MC Lyte, Rakim & KRS-One, who begat Black Thought, Pharoahe Monch, Mos Def & Jean Grae, who begat Rapsody, Noname, Chance & this moment & renaissance in poetic cultural work.
>
> First and foremost it was her bars. Her dedication to the line and craft. Her syllabilistics & music. The song she squeezed from language. Nothing wasted, each utterance essential. Her gaze, the permission she gave to generations to record what was in front of their nose or in the alleys behind us.
>
> It was her commitment to the people. The classes she held in church, the work she did with the Blackstone Rangers, the thou-

sands of young people she mentored, encouraged to dream a new reality. The thousands of dollars he pulled from her own pocket to pay young poets. The capacity to interact with so many, to listen and witness and grow generations of cannon builders and aesthetic revolutionaries.

Ms. Brooks was a poet and a teacher. Haki Madhubuti is a poet and a teacher. KRS-ONE is a poet and a teacher. I am because they are.

I tell stories of the city I see and the city I hope we can become. I listen to the thousands of stories from young writers in every zip code on a yearly basis because Ms. Brooks and Studs Terkel listen. And this too is the work. The desire to hear and hear anew and to hear the voices that have been systematically denied agency and center-space in the civic discourse. To hold and carve and build space for those voices, to ensure they are heard and championed and cultivated because that is what democracy means, what community is, and what the work of the poet became in the body and living example of Ms. Brooks, a dedicated craftsperson who built a new literature and opened the door for the many to participate and re-inscribe and imagine who we are, have been and who we will become.

This streamlined version of Gwendolyn's continuity through generations gives some sense of her enormous impact on black poetry today that is not of the academy. Young people are finding their voices and visions through her voice and vision. She is still as relevant today to young rappers as she was to the Black Arts poets of the 1960s. Poet and Brooks scholar Quraysh Ali Lansana clarifies Brooks's relationship with rap and young people.

Miss Brooks was not a big fan of Hip-Hop/Rap (though she appreciated Rap as a poetic form and marveled at the linguistic and lyrical prowess of many emcees). She was not an admirer of profanity, considering swear words reflect of "a poverty of imagination."

One evening during workshop she assigned the eleven of us the task of creating original insults without including curse words.

Miss Brooks did appreciate the subject matter of most conscious rap, which focused on the struggles and triumphs of black life. This is not surprising, as the overwhelming majority of her work is consumed with the details and politics of the black experience.

Children Coming Home, the 1991 volume she self-published (likely the only Pulitzer Prize recipient to self-publish) is a book of persona poems in the voices of children she met when she adopted Jenner Elementary School in the late 1980's. Jenner served students who lived in the troubled Cabrini-Green Housing Projects, a failed social living experiment riddled with civic neglect, gang violence and crack. These are, in fact, the reasons she volunteered her time to work with young people at Jenner.

The poems in *Children Coming Home* are raw, intimate and often disturbing. They are what N.W.A. called "reality rap." These poems are Miss Brooks as an in-your-face emcee. The poems look you in the eye and dare you to flinch.

When asked in an online survey to choose poets who had influenced them, some poets chose Audre Lorde or young poets. Malcolm London, the Chicago rapper and activist, chose Gwendolyn Brooks. Her "Beverly Hills, Chicago" had changed his point of view, had changed his way of looking at the world as he lived in an impoverished black community and went to school in a wealthy white community. After reading Gwendolyn, he understood his own dilemma better. She has a way of helping people understand.

Another legendary poet, Mari Evans, exhorted the Black Arts Movement poets to "Speak the Truth to the People." This was always true of Gwendolyn. She spoke the truth even when it went against the grain. And she taught by excellent example.

Two Gwendolyn Brooks scholars offered perspectives on her a year after her death, October 30, 2001. In the *Chicago Tribune*, Dr. B. J. Bolden said, "In the popular world, she is a hero of the community.

People see her as an ordinary person who really was extraordinary. She claimed to be humble. She wanted to be with the people. But she was a monumental role figure. She heightened awareness of the need for community."

Dr. D. H. Melhem said, "In the devastations of September 11, and their relentless aftermath, such questions of values loom larger than ever. . . . Her legacy is to extend the boundaries of the human heart."

Gwendolyn Brooks, daughter, sister, wife, mother, friend, mentor to many, poet, black woman poet and writer continues in each of us who is touched by her work and by memories of her. That compassionate and gifted black woman who cast such a dazzling glow is truly immortal.

Acknowledgments

My gratitude to my editor, Rakia Clark, for offering this project to me and giving me the freedom and help in bringing it to fruition. To Beacon Press for honoring Gwendolyn Brooks in the centennial year of her birth and giving me the privilege of writing her biography. To Dr. Jacqueline Goldsby for suggesting me for the work of biographer to my poetic role model.

For encouragement and support: my brothers, George Jr. and Prentiss J. Jackson.

And my sisters, Margaret Jackson Stewart, Betty Jackson Uzzell, Sharon Jackson Sanders, and Delores Jackson Wolfley.

Literary angels, sister Rosemary Jackson Lawson and sister-friend Sarah Odishoo.

A special thank you to Quraysh and Emily Lansana.

To all my nieces and nephews.

And my research associate and sister-friend Roella Davis.

And Rose Perkins of Third World Press

And Kathleen Bethel, librarian at Northwestern University.

And to the contributors of the last chapter.

Thanks and praise.

Notes

I obtained invaluable details from Gwendolyn Brooks's *Report from Part One* and *Report from Part Two* and from George Kent's *A Life of Gwendolyn Brooks*, as well as from personal interviews conducted and correspondence in 2016 with Nora Brooks Blakely, Kevin Coval, Reginald Gibbons, Patricia Spears Jones, Renee Knox, Emily Lansana, Quraysh Ali Lansana, Haki R. Madhubuti, Useni Eugene Perkins, Dr. Ann Smith, Bryant Smith, and Val Gray Ward. Dr. Clovis E. Semmes afforded me archives from the *Chicago Defender*. The guidance and aid of the Gwendolyn Brooks archival staff at the University of Illinois Library is appreciated with all their assistance.

CHAPTER 1: "GRANT ME A VOICE, AND SPEAKING EYES"
1. Brooks, *Report from Part One*, 57.
2. Ibid.
3. Ibid., 37–38.
4. Kent, *A Life of Gwendolyn Brooks*, 25.
5. Ibid., 36.
6. Stetson, "Songs After Sunset," 121.
7. Kent, *A Life of Gwendolyn Brooks*, 18.
8. Ibid., 41.
9. Ibid., 41.
10. Brooks, *Report from Part One*, 190.
11. Kent, *A Life of Gwendolyn Brooks*, 43.
12. James R. Grossman, *Land of Hope: Chicago, Black Southerners, and the Great Migration* (Chicago: University of Chicago Press, 1989), 130.

CHAPTER 2: VISIONARIES

1. Kent, *A Life of Gwendolyn Brooks*, 51.
2. Brooks, *Report from Part One*, 69.
3. Brooks, "How I Think Poetry Should Be Written With an Original Poem," September 11, 1938, in Brooks archive, Bancroft Library, University of California, Berkekely.
4. Brooks, *Report from Part One*, 66.
5. Semmes, *The Regal Theater and Black Culture*, 95.
6. Ibid., 112.
7. Black, *Bridges of Memory*, 74.
8. Brooks, *Report from Part One*, 68.
9. Ibid., 69.
10. Ibid., photo insert, 12.
11. Ibid., 71.
12. Richard Wright to Edward C. Aswell, September 18, 1944, Harper & Row author files, Princeton University Library. All quotations from Harper & Row correspondence from 1944 to 1958 are quoted by permission of Harper and Row and Princeton University Library.
13. Brooks, *Report from Part One*, 72.

CHAPTER 3: A LIGHT AND DIPLOMATIC BIRD

1. Bone and Courage, *Muse in Bronzeville*, 172.
2. Ibid.
3. Ibid., 174.
4. Brooks, *Report from Part One*, 155.
5. Kent, *A Life of Gwendolyn Brooks*, 74–75.

CHAPTER 4: HITTING HER STRIDE

1. Ibid., 76.
2. Brooks, *Report from Part One*, 158.
3. Genevieve Taggard to Elizabeth Lawrence, July 1948, Harper & Row author files.
4. Elizabeth Lawrence to Gwendolyn Brooks, July 14, 1948, Harper & Row author files.
5. Kent, *A Life of Gwendolyn Brooks*, 78.
6. Elizabeth Lawrence to Gwendolyn Brooks, March 3, 1949, Harper & Row author files; Gwendolyn Brooks to Elizabeth Lawrence, March 11.2, 1949, Harper & Row author files.
7. Kent, *A Life of Gwendolyn Brooks*, 87–88.

CHAPTER 5: A PULITZER IS A SMILE

1. Gwendolyn Brooks, Aida Aronoff, WNET Creative Persons Series.

2. Gwendolyn Brooks to Elizabeth Lawrence, May 1950, Harper & Row author files.

3. Brooks, *Report from Part One*, 146.

4. Kent, *A Life of Gwendolyn Brooks*, 95–96.

5. Gwendolyn Brooks to Langston Hughes, December 11, 1951, Harper & Row author files.

6. Kent, *A Life of Gwendolyn Brooks*, 93.

7. *Phylon*, Special Issue, The Negro in Literature (1950): 312.

8. Kent, *A Life of Gwendolyn Brooks*, 103.

9. Brooks, *Report from Part One*, 162.

10. Ibid., 192.

11. Ann Petry to Elizabeth Lawrence, June 11, 1953, Harper & Row author files.

12. Inez Stark Boulton to Elizabeth Lawrence, November 3, 1953, Harper & Row author files.

13. Gwendolyn Brooks to Elizabeth Lawrence, April 7, 1958, Harper & Row author files.

14. Brooks, *Report from Part One*, 193.

15. Elizabeth Lawrence to Gwendolyn Brooks, February 9, 1959, Harper & Row author files.

16. Kent, *A Life of Gwendolyn Brooks*, 94.

17. Brooks, *Report from Part One*, 78.

18. Kent, *A Life of Gwendolyn Brooks*, 168.

19. Brooks, *Report from Part One*, 78.

CHAPTER 6: BLACK IS BEAUTIFUL

1. Kent, *A Life of Gwendolyn Brooks*, 192.

2. Ibid., 154.

3. Ibid., 199.

4. Ibid., 200.

5. Brooks, *Report from Part One*, 85.

6. Ibid., 85.

7. Ibid., 169.

8. *Ebony*, December 23, 1967, 48–50

9. Elizabeth Lawrence to Gwendolyn Brooks, August 29, 1962, Harper & Row author files.

10. Brooks, *Report from Part One*, 152.

11. Hoyt W. Fuller to Gwendolyn Brooks, January 9, 1968, Brooks archive.

12. Brooks, *Report from Part One*, 152.

CHAPTER 7: A SURPRISED QUEENHOOD

1. Kent, *A Life of Gwendolyn Brooks*, 191.

2. *Chicago Defender*, May 8, 1965.

3. *Chicago Defender*, January 8, 1968.

4. Don Lee to Gwendolyn Brooks, July 1971, Brooks archive.

5. "Tanzania, Africa: A Panther in Anusha," *Talking Drum*, www.thetalking drum.com/bpp3.html, accessed January 19, 2017.

6. W. E. B. Du Bois, "Of Our Spiritual Strivings," *The Souls of Black Folks* (Chicago: A. C. McClurg, 1903), http://www.bartleby.com/114/1.html.

7. Brooks, *Report from Part Two*, 59.

8. Archive note January 31, 1971.

9. Ibid.

10. Brooks, *Report from Part One*, 197.

11. Ibid.

CHAPTER 8: JOURNEYS

1. Brooks, *Report from Part One*, 58.

2. "Conversation," *Essence*, April 1971.

3. Brooks, *Report from Part One*, 179.

4. Brooks, *Report from Part Two*, 47–48.

5. Ibid., 48.

6. Ibid., 51.

7. Kennedy, *An Introduction to Poetry*, 292.

8. Brooks, *Report from Part Two*, 21–28.

9. Ibid., 53.

10. Ibid., 58–60.

11. Ibid., 64–65.

12. Ibid., 77-78.

CHAPTER 9: BLACKS

1. Gwendolyn Brooks to Betty Owens, June 1, 1987, archives.

2. Brooks archive.

3. Ta-Nehisi Coates, "My President Was Black," *Atlantic*, January/February 2017.

4. Brooks, *Report from Part Two*, 127.

5. Ibid., 141.

CHAPTER 10: IMMORTALITY OF A KIND

1. Madhubuti, *Honoring Genius*, 57–58, 60.

Selected Bibliography

Black, Jr., Timuel D. *Bridges of Memory*. Evanston/Chicago: Northwestern University Press/DuSable Museum of African American History, 2003.

Bone, Robert, and Richard A. Courage. *The Muse in Bronzeville: African American Creative Expression in Chicago, 1932–1955*. New Brunswick, NJ: Rutgers University Press, 2011.

Brooks, Gwendolyn. *Blacks*. Chicago: The David Company, 1987.

Brooks, Gwendolyn. *Primer for Blacks*. Chicago: Third World Press, 1980.

Brooks, Gwendolyn. *Report from Part One*. Detroit: Broadside Press, 1972.

Brooks, Gwendolyn. *Report from Part Two*. Chicago: Third World Press, 1996.

Brooks, Gwendolyn. *to disembark*. Chicago: Third World Press, 1981.

Bryant, Jacqueline Imani, ed. *Gwendolyn Brooks and Working Writers*. Chicago: Third World Press, 2007.

Guzman, Richard R., ed. *Black Writing from Chicago*. Carbondale: Southern Illinois University Press, 2006.

Harper, Michael S., and Anthony Walton, eds. *The Vintage Book of African American Poetry*. New York: Vintage Books, 2000.

Jackson, Lawrence P. *The Indignant Generation: A Narrative History of African American Writers and Critics 1934–1960*. Princeton, NJ: Princeton University Press, 2011.

Kennedy, X. J., ed. *An Introduction to Poetry, Seventh Edition*. Glenview, IL: Scott Foresman and Co., 1990.

Kent, George E. *A Life of Gwendolyn Brooks*. Lexington: University Press of Kentucky, 1990.

Madhubuti, Haki R. *Honoring Genius, Gwendolyn Brooks: The Narrative of Craft, Art, Kindness and Justice*. Chicago: Third World Press, 2011.

Melhem, D. H. *Gwendolyn Brooks, Poetry and the Heroic Voice*. Lexington: University Press of Kentucky. 1987

Moore, Natalie Y. *The South Side*. New York: St. Martin's Press, 2016.

Semmes, Clovis E. *The Regal Theater and Black Culture*. New York: Palgrave Mac-Millan, 2006.

Stetson, Erline. "Songs After Sunset (1935–1936): The Unpublished Poetry of Gwendolyn Brooks." In *A Life Distilled: Gwendolyn Brooks, Her Poetry and Fiction*, edited by Maria K. Mootry and Gary Smith. Urbana: University of Illinois Press, 1989.

Tate, Claudia, ed. *Black Women Writers at Work*. New York: Continuum, 1983

Tracey, Steven, ed. *Writers of the Black Chicago Renaissance*. Urbana: University of Illinois Press, 2012.

Travis, Dempsey. *An Autobiography of Black Chicago*. Chicago: Bolden Books, 2013.

OTHER SOURCES

Aronoff, Aida. *Gwendolyn Brooks*. WNET Creative Persons Series, US, 16mm, 29 min., 1966.

Articles on Gwendolyn Brooks, *Chicago Defender*, 1938–1975, downloaded March 17, 2016. www.thetalkingdrum.com/bpp3.html.